HISTORY 3
FOR YOUNG CATHOLICS

The Catholic Faith
Comes to the Americas

WRITTEN BY
SETON STAFF

SETON PRESS
FRONT ROYAL, VA

Executive Editor: Dr. Mary Kay Clark
Editors: Seton Staff

© 2019 Seton Home Study School
All rights reserved.
Printed in the United States of America

Seton Home Study School
1350 Progress Drive
Front Royal, VA 22630
Phone: (540) 636-9990
Fax: (540) 636-1602

For more information, visit us on the Web at www.setonhome.org
Contact us by e-mail at info@setonhome.org

ISBN: 978-1-60704-081-1

Cover: *Stained glass window from the Shrine of St. John Neumann, Philadelphia*

DEDICATED TO THE SACRED HEART OF JESUS

TABLE OF CONTENTS

Overview of the Text

The Catholic Faith Comes to the Americas was written for third graders as an introduction to American history. We include short biographies of American Catholics who influenced our society in many ways. They not only strengthened the Catholic Faith in America, but also believed in the principle of freedom.

We encourage enrichment with map and globe work, as well as additional reading about the Catholics in this book. The Internet is a resource that you and your child can use to see additional images as well as videos. Some of the adventure of these stories, such as the sea battles, can help young children appreciate the difficulties of those who fought for American freedom. The images and videos on the Internet bring home the reality of the bravery of our American heroes.

We hope you can visit the library once a week to obtain supplemental books related to the lessons. Libraries often have book sales, and you may be able to purchase reference books and atlases. Consider using an encyclopedia with your child in order to research the events and people mentioned in the book.

Please note that the Answer Key is located in the back of the book.

We hope you and your child enjoy this book.

Introduction

Faith, obedience, charity, humility, and a zeal to serve God were among the reasons some Catholics left their homes in Europe to help spread the Catholic Faith in the Americas. These Catholics traveled to an unknown land to follow Christ's call: "Go and teach all nations." The great work they began in the New World should be known to all Catholics who live in America today.

Many of the blessings we take for granted today exist because hardworking and faithful Catholics suffered and sacrificed. They built many of the churches, schools, hospitals, and orphanages that we have today. Good priests, nuns, brothers, and parents were God's tools to build a strong and lasting Catholic faith in the Americas. With God's help, the Catholic faith will endure, grow, and be instrumental in making the United States a truly Christian nation.

Catholics settled most of Central and South America, including Mexico. These Catholics traveled from the European countries of Spain and Portugal. In North America, the French settled in what is now Canada and Louisiana. The Spanish settled in Florida, California, and the Southwest. What is now the eastern United States of America was settled mostly by English, Dutch, German, and French Protestants. Catholics who dared

St. John Neumann, pray for us.

to go to these areas were persecuted. Over the years, however, Catholics moved into these areas as well. Today, many eastern coast areas of the United States have large Catholic populations. In fact, the United States is almost 25% Catholic.

The Faith these Catholic immigrants brought to the Americas has been handed down to each new generation. Catholic men and women possibly taught and helped our grandparents and great-grandparents.

We should thank those who came before us. Through their determination and example, we can learn the value of hard work and prayer.

Mary, Mother of the Church, pray for us.

1

Chapter 1

St. Brendan
The Navigator

Words to Remember

habit: a uniform type of clothing worn by members of religious orders

monk: a male religious who lives in prayerful community in a monastery

founder: a person who starts a new religious community

rule: written rules by which men or women live in a religious community

piety: a deep respect for God and holy things, and a prayerful attitude

ordain: to make a man a deacon, priest, or bishop through the sacrament of Holy Orders

monastery: a dwelling place where monks or nuns live a community life of prayer and work

barren: lifeless; lacking plants and crops

tradition: a long-standing belief passed down from past generations

Places to Remember

North Atlantic: ocean between Europe and North America

Ireland: island country west of Europe and England

Tralee: city on the west coast of Ireland

People to Remember

Brig: founder of a women's religious order; sister of St. Brendan

St. Brendan: Irish monk who may have discovered America

St. Brendan's early life

About five hundred years after the death and resurrection of Jesus Christ, two children were born to the McFinlugh family: Brendan and his sister Brig. They lived in Tralee on the west coast of Ireland. The sea and sailing were a natural part of Brendan's life as a boy. He loved to sail with his father.

Brendan was a good and obedient son. His father taught him the catechism and he saw his son growing in holiness. He decided to send Brendan to Bishop Erc to be trained and educated in God's ways. Mr. McFinlugh hoped that Brendan would find a way to serve God.

Brendan learned quickly. He worked hard and prayed that God would show him what to do with his life. Bishop Erc advised Brendan to become a priest. Brendan decided he wanted to be a priest. After a few years, the bishop ordained Brendan.

Brendan becomes a priest and monk

When Brendan was ordained a priest of God, he also became a monk. He then founded an order of monks at the city of Clonfert, in Ireland. One tradition teaches that an angel gave Brendan the rule for his order. It is believed that the night before Brendan was ordained, an angel appeared to him. Brendan asked, "What does God want me to do?"

The angel replied, "You are to found an order of monks. They will pray for the spread of the faith of Christ. That faith must spread throughout the world. More things are done by prayer than anyone knows."

Prayer and work became the basis of St. Brendan's rule for his monks. One kind of work that was done by Irish monks was to copy and illustrate Bibles. These were called illuminated manuscripts. One of the most famous books of the Gospels is called the Book of Kells, and it was copied and illustrated by a group of Irish monks around the year 800.

Illuminated Manuscript

Brendan's Order grows

The angel also told Brendan to encourage his sister Brig to found an order of nuns. Brendan talked to Brig and she did establish an order at a place called Enach Duin. The nuns prayed for the spread of the Church throughout the world and grew their own food on the land around their monastery. The nuns were very pious. Their reputation of holiness spread throughout Ireland.

The monks in Brendan's order became known for their piety and holiness. The number of young men following Brendan's good example increased each year. One monastery could no longer hold all the monks. Still more men wanted to join Brendan's Order of monks.

Brendan decided to build new monasteries

Brendan decided to sail to several islands in the North Atlantic Ocean where he could build new

The bishop blesses St. Brendan.

monasteries. Brendan and many monks built a boat to travel to some of the islands. There was a crucifix, altar, and tabernacle on the boat. Mass was to be offered each day while on their search at sea. The monks would live on the boat as if they were still in their own monastery.

Finally, the boat was ready to sail. Before they set sail, Brendan blessed the boat. Early one morning, Brendan and his monks said goodbye to the other monks. Then they walked on board the floating "monastery."

As Brendan and his monks sailed in their "monastery" ship around the islands in the North Atlantic Ocean, Saint Brendan kept a diary about the sea voyage. At that time, no one knew how big the world was. Brendan's writings, which tell about the long sea journey, was of great interest to the people of Ireland.

The monks sailed on and on for at least three months. Some people believe the trip could have been much longer, perhaps even several years. Their Catholic Faith gave the monks the courage to continue their voyage. Finally, the monks found land.

Did Brendan reach North America?

Some people believe that Brendan sailed across the Atlantic Ocean and reached the shores of America. It is possible that Brendan's route was later followed by the Vikings.

Brendan and the monks spent some time in this strange new "world" across the ocean. However, Brendan and his monks found the new land too cold and barren to support life. Not many plants grew there. Vegetables would not grow. So they decided to sail back home to Ireland. Before they left the new land, however, St. Brendan prayed, "One day, may this land know Christ's Church."

St. Brendan blesses the monks as they set sail.

The last days of St. Brendan

When Brendan returned home, he visited his sister Brig. She was very happy to see her brother once again. She saw that he did not look well. Brendan was very tired after his long journey to and from the new land. He needed rest.

After a few days, Brig saw that Brendan was very sick. Brig prayed that if Brendan's work on Earth was finished, God would take him home to Heaven. The next day Brendan died.

St. Brendan's feast day, May 16, is celebrated throughout Ireland.

St. Brendan, pray for us.

Do You Remember?

1. Where did St. Brendan live? _____

2. How long did it take St. Brendan and his monks to reach the cold land as

   they sailed west? _____

3. What was St. Brendan's prayer for this new land? _____

   _____

   _____

Map Study Skills

1. On a globe or atlas, find the two islands of Ireland and England, just west of

   the European continent. (Hint: Look two lines north of the equator.)

2. Name the ocean Brendan crossed from Ireland to the Americas.

   _____

A modern copy of St. Brendan's boat

6

Chapter 2

The Discovery of the Americas

Words to Remember

valiantly: with great courage

corrupt: having an evil influence; to decay

cargo: things carried on ships from one place to another

plank: a long strip of wood on a ship's deck

horizon: the farthest point of land or sea visible in the distance

invaders: a hostile group of people who enter a foreign land to make war on the people living there

monarchs: kings and queens who rule a country

Places to Remember

Europe: continent to the northeast of the Atlantic Ocean

Africa: continent to the southeast of the Atlantic Ocean

Portugal: country in the southern part of Europe, west of Spain on the Atlantic Ocean

Spain: country in the southern part of Europe, east of Portugal and north of the Mediterranean Sea

Indies: the islands around India which Columbus was trying to reach

Mediterranean Sea: body of water bounded by Europe on the north side, Africa on the south, and Asia on the east

People to Remember

Christopher Columbus: the Catholic explorer who, in 1492, discovered a new continent called the New World, later named America

Queen Isabella and King Ferdinand: Catholic queen and king of Spain who gave Columbus the ships he needed to sail west

Moors: Muslims from North Africa who invaded Spain

Muslims: those who follow the false religion started by a man named Mohammed

Columbus and Isabella

St. Brendan had prayed that Christ's Church would come to the strange new world he discovered. About one thousand years after his prayer, two persons were born who would be the answer to his prayers. They were born hundreds of miles apart, but one day they would meet and change the world as they knew it. These two people were Christopher Columbus and Queen Isabella of Spain. Columbus and Isabella were very different. Yet one thing they had in common was a great love for the Catholic Church.

Queen Isabella grows up

Queen Isabella was born into the royal house of Castile, a part of Spain. Isabella's father died when she was only three years old. As a result, she grew up at the royal court of her brother, King Henry IV.

Young Christopher Columbus

Christopher Columbus grew up in Genoa, Italy, a small seaport on the Mediterranean Sea. His father was a weaver, but Columbus had no interest in weaving. He loved the sea. Each day, he would go down to the docks and watch the ships unload the cargo from the East. He talked to the sailors about their adventures at sea. He was able to learn where the ships had been and where they were going.

Columbus talked to the sailors about their adventures.

When you look at a map today, you see North and South America to the west of Europe. Maps at the time of Columbus, however, showed only the "Sea of Darkness" to the west of Europe. No one knew what was beyond the western horizon of Europe. People were afraid of the unknown sea area.

At the age of fourteen, Christopher Columbus sailed on his first ship. The ship sailed around the Mediterranean Sea. Columbus learned how to handle a ship. He worked hard on ships, and prayed that someday God would give him a ship of his own to command.

Several years later, Columbus was asked to sail a ship to England. For the first time, Columbus sailed out of the quiet safety of the Mediterranean Sea. He sailed into the Atlantic Ocean to reach England. Even though the ocean's waters were rough and sometimes had high waves, Columbus handled the ship well. The sailors had trust in the young sea captain.

Just off the coast of Portugal, however, pirates attacked the ship. The sailors fought valiantly. Despite their efforts, however, the ship split apart and sank. Columbus, holding on to one of the ship's planks that was floating in the water, was washed ashore in Portugal.

The finest map makers were in Portugal.

Portugal had the world's finest sailors and map makers

In those days, the finest ships in the world were made in Portugal. In Portugal were many of the finest map makers of the time. Some people think God wanted Christopher Columbus to learn more about ships and maps in the shipping school of Portugal.

Columbus studied the maps he saw in Portugal. He was a very good student. He came to believe that the Earth is round. He thought, "If the world is really round like a ball, and I sail west across the Atlantic Ocean, I can reach India by sea. Then our merchants can reach India much faster than traveling east over the lands of Europe." At that time, Europe carried on trade with India but products were often expensive because of the long overland trip.

Christopher Columbus needed ships, sailors, and supplies to prove he could reach the east (India) by sailing west. So Columbus went to Spain for help. There he met Queen Isabella.

Columbus meets Isabella and King Ferdinand.

Princess Isabella

Before Isabella became queen, the people living in the royal castles in which she grew up were very dishonest and corrupt. Leaders acted out of a desire for money and power rather than to help the citizens. People tried to use Isabella to gain power and money for themselves. However, Isabella was a good Catholic who went to daily Mass and Communion. She said special prayers each day that God would protect her country of Spain and keep her free from serious sin. Isabella went to confession often.

Isabella's grandmother taught her to cook, sew, and ride a horse. When she was eighteen, Isabella married Prince Ferdinand of Aragon. Aragon was a large kingdom in Spain. Ferdinand and Isabella loved each other very much. Even though she was a princess, Isabella mended her husband's shirts and made his socks.

Isabella becomes Queen

When Isabella's brother died, Isabella became Queen of Castile, the other large kingdom in Spain. She inherited a great deal of money. Isabella used her money to stop the fighting and do away with the evil activities in the royal court. She set up a local police force in each town to protect its citizens. She appointed good Catholic judges to the town courts.

Isabella made sure that even the poorest Spanish peasant would be given respect and rights. Every citizen was treated fairly. At times, she herself went to local courts. Queen Isabella even sat through some court hearings to make sure that the judge's decisions were just and fair.

Part of Isabella's country was controlled by the Moors. The Moors were Muslims from North Africa. They had invaded Spain hundreds of years before Isabella was born. She wanted to free her country from these non-Christian invaders. She wanted to make it a Catholic country again.

Then Ferdinand's father died. Ferdinand became the king of Aragon. This united the two kingdoms of Castile and Aragon. Spain was now one country. Now Isabella and Ferdinand had the men and money to fight the invading Moors. They would drive the Moors out of Spain and back to Africa.

Ferdinand and Isabella drove the Moors out of Spain in 1492.

Columbus and Isabella meet

When Columbus visited the Spanish court, Isabella and Ferdinand were busy fighting to free Spain from the Moors. Columbus impressed Isabella. She believed he was a man of vision and determination, as well as a good Catholic. Isabella was a good judge of people. Just the year before, she had appointed a poor, humble, unknown Franciscan priest named Juan Perez to help the priests to be more holy. Fr. Perez did his job very well and helped other priests to say more devout Masses and hear more confessions. Unfortunately, because of the war, the king and queen could not pay for the long journey Columbus would be making across the ocean. Isabella told him to come back when the war was over.

Columbus was discouraged. He wanted to start his sea journey right away. He decided to seek help in France. On his way to France, Columbus met Fr. Perez. The priest listened carefully to Columbus' plan to sail west to find the Indies. He knew instantly how important such a trip could be.

"Go back to the court," said Fr. Perez. "Tell the queen I sent you. I will go to see her myself. I will tell her you must sail through the Sea of Darkness. If you can find a shortcut to India, Spain will become a very great country. More importantly, Spain can send missionaries to India."

After a couple of weeks, Fr. Perez visited Isabella. He told her that this was an opportunity to send missionaries to the East. They could convert the people living there. The missionaries would spread the good news of Jesus around the world.

Father Perez spoke with Isabella about Columbus.

Isabella listened to Fr. Perez and his ideas. She loved her Catholic Faith. She knew in her heart that this was what God wanted Spain to do.

Isabella gives Columbus the money for his journey

In 1492, the long war against the Moors finally ended. Ferdinand and Isabella gave Columbus the money for his journey to India. He and his sailors traveled in three ships: the *Niña*, the *Pinta*, and the *Santa Maria*. He set out to find a way to the East Indies, which are a group of islands near India.

Columbus wanted to fulfill Isabella's dream to send missionaries to the East. He hoped to convert the people living there to the Catholic Church. Columbus was sailing for God and for Spain.

The three tiny ships sailed west for two months. By that time, the sailors had grown discouraged and afraid. They complained bitterly. They wanted to turn back. Columbus urged them to be brave. He prayed that God would help them.

The *Nina*, the *Pinta*, and the *Santa Maria* set sail.

Columbus discovers America

Columbus kept a diary on his voyage. In it, he wrote that if he did not see land by the Feast of Our Lady of the Pillar, an important Spanish feast day, he would turn the ships back. Finally, early on the morning of October 12, 1492, the Feast of Our Lady of the Pillar, a sailor saw land.

"Land ho! Land ho!" the sailor shouted. When Columbus sighted the land, the priests on his ships asked that everyone kneel down and pray to Our Lord and Our Lady of the Pillar in thanksgiving.

As soon as Columbus landed, he claimed the land for Spain. He called the land "San Salvador," which means "Holy Savior" in Spanish. The sailors thanked God for bringing them safely to land. Columbus thought he had found the East Indies near India. He called the people he found there "Indians."

In later years, Columbus made three more trips. He always believed he had reached islands off the coast of Asia.

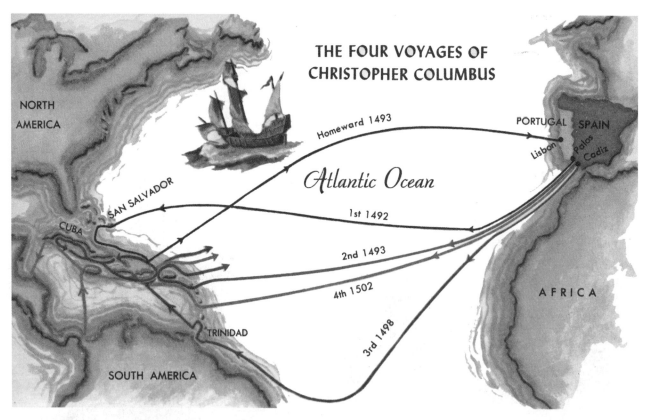

Why we live in "America"

Later another explorer named Amerigo Vespucci made a journey to the New World. When he returned to Spain, Amerigo wrote of the journey. A German mapmaker heard these stories. The mapmaker thought Amerigo had discovered the New World. Therefore, when he drew his maps, he called the land "America," after Amerigo. Other mapmakers did the same. That is why today we live in America and not Columbia!

Do You Remember?

1. What were the names of the three ships of Christopher Columbus?

   _____, _____, and _____

2. Who were the king and queen who helped Christopher Columbus?

   _____ and _____

3. What did Christopher Columbus call the place which he landed?

   _____

Map Study Skills

1. Locate the line above the equator. It is the Tropic of Cancer.

2. Locate the Mediterranean Sea, which is surrounded by Europe on the north and Africa on the south.

Columbus discovers America

Chapter 3

The Conversion of Mexico

Words to Remember

Nahuatl: the language of the Aztecs

Aztecs: one of the Indian groups that lived in Mexico

conquistador: a Spanish soldier in America

persist: to keep trying

Places to Remember

Pacific Ocean: the body of water west of North and South America

Isthmus of Panama: the narrow strip of land connecting North and South America

England: island country in northern Europe

Genoa: port in northwest Italy

People to Remember

Vasco Balboa: found the Pacific Ocean

John Cabot: sailed to North America for England

Hernan Cortes: conquered Mexico

Juan Diego: Indian who saw Our Lady of Guadalupe

Bishop Zumarraga: the first bishop of Mexico

Mexico City Cathedral

Other explorers come to the New World

Soon word of the discovery of Christopher Columbus reached England. The English king hired John Cabot, a captain from Genoa, to sail west. John Cabot sailed west, but farther north than Columbus. He landed in North America. England later claimed North America as her land since John Cabot discovered it.

Meanwhile, Spanish explorers started sailing to America. The Indians told Vasco Balboa, a Spanish conquistador, about a large body of water to the west of America. So Vasco Balboa walked across the Isthmus of Panama. There he found the Pacific Ocean. Now people began to realize that what Columbus had discovered was a whole new continent, almost like a new world.

Hernan Cortes comes to Mexico

In 1519, Hernan Cortes, another Spanish explorer, went to the area we now call Mexico. Hernan Cortes tried to make a trade agreement between Spain and the Aztec people who lived there.

The Aztecs had built cities, but they were not civilized. The Aztecs killed people in their "temples."

Cortes went to Tenochtitlan, the main Aztec city, where he was greeted by Montezuma, the Aztec emperor. One night, several months later, while Cortes was out of the city, a foolish soldier named Alvarado attacked a crowd of Aztecs during one of their pagan religious ceremonies. The Spanish soldiers killed a number of the "worshipers." In anger, the Aztecs killed many of the Spaniard soldiers and drove the others out of the city.

Cortes meets Montezuma

When he returned, Cortes and his men took refuge in a friendly Indian village. When they recovered, they attacked the Aztecs and destroyed most of the city of Tenochtitlan.

Cortes and his soldiers were especially angry about the Aztec practice of human sacrifice. The Spanish attack put an end to the practice of human sacrifice, that is, murdering people in an offering to false gods. Cortes then set up a government based on Catholic Spanish law. Later Cortes rebuilt the city of Tenochtitlan, and renamed it Mexico City. Then Cortes brought priests from Spain to teach the Indians about the one true God and about the Catholic Faith.

The Spanish attack put an end to human sacrifice.

Juan Diego grows up in Mexico

The priests found it hard to convert the Aztecs. The Aztecs did not believe in God. Very few of the Indians were converted to the Catholic Faith. One of the first persons converted was an older, humble Indian who was baptized as Juan Diego.

As a boy of only thirteen years old, before the arrival of Cortes, Juan Diego may have seen the "Night of Darkness." On that terrible night, the Aztec rulers killed over 80,000 Aztec Indian prisoners. They were killed in the Aztec temple. Many Aztecs knew this was wrong, and many suffered as family members and friends were killed. Juan knew these things were terribly wrong. He hoped there was a better way to live but he didn't know what anyone could do.

Juan Diego is baptized

Then came the Franciscan priests, who spoke of Christ's love for all of us. The Franciscan priests told the Indians about how Jesus Christ sacrificed His life for all mankind. God blessed Juan with the gift of faith. Juan, his wife, and his uncle were converted to the Catholic Faith. The Franciscan priests needed help if they were going to succeed in converting the other Indians. Help was coming.

The Blessed Mother Mary always chooses the poorest, most humble, and most faithful people to be her messengers. The loving, caring Juan Diego fit that description.

Juan, after his conversion, walked miles to Mass every morning. His faith was strong. His love of Jesus Christ in the Blessed Sacrament was great. The glow of holiness could be seen on Juan's wrinkled face. He was now over fifty years old.

The Blessed Mother appears to Juan Diego

One day while walking over the hill to Mexico City, Juan heard a beautiful voice. He looked and saw a strange white cloud. There was a rainbow around it. Suddenly, a young lady appeared in front of the cloud. Her clothes were shining brightly. The intense light made everything around the cloud look like jewels.

Juan Diego saw a strange white cloud.

Juan suddenly knew the Lady was from Heaven. He fell on his knees in front of the beautiful Lady. "Where are you going?" she asked. Though Juan was afraid, he answered, "I am going down the hill. I go to Mass in Mexico City every day."

The Lady smiled. "I am the Virgin Mary, Mother of God. I want a church built here on this hill in my honor," she said. "I love all men, both Indian and Spanish. I will bless all of Mexico if my wishes are granted. Juan, I want you to go to Bishop Zumarraga. You will give him my message."

Juan hurried to the bishop's house. When he arrived, the guards would not let him enter, but Juan was persistent. Finally, the bishop saw the poor, unknown Indian. "Come back later," Bishop Zumarraga said. Obediently, Juan hurried back to the Lady. She was waiting for him.

Juan said, "Dear Lady, you must find someone more important to speak to the bishop. He will not listen to a poor Indian like me."

Our Lady replied, "Juan, you must be my messenger. You can convince the bishop to do as I wish. Will you go again tomorrow?"

Juan answered, "Yes, my Lady." Then he went home.

The next day, Sunday, December 10, Juan went to Mass. Then he went to the bishop's house. The guards tried to stop him. Juan was quite persistent, and succeeded in meeting the bishop.

Juan told the bishop what the beautiful Lady wanted. The bishop said, "Is what you are telling me true? I need proof. Tell the Lady to send proof that she is the Virgin Mary, Mother of God."

On his way home, Juan stopped at the hill. The Lady was waiting. She asked Juan, "What did the bishop say?" Juan replied, "The bishop wants proof that you are the Virgin Mary, Mother of God."

The Lady smiled and said, "Come back tomorrow. I will give you proof the bishop will believe." So Juan hurried home as it was getting dark.

The Blessed Mother performs a miracle

The next day, Juan's uncle was very sick. Juan had to stay home and care for his uncle. As the day wore on, the uncle became seriously ill. The uncle thought he was going to die.

The uncle said, "Juan, please bring me a priest." Juan replied, "It is dark. I cannot go outside now. I will go tomorrow."

As dawn broke on December 12, 1531, Juan left to find a priest. Juan walked all the way around the hill. He was ashamed because he had not returned the day before to meet the Lady. To his surprise, the Lady suddenly appeared and came down the hill to meet him.

She said, "Don't worry, Juan. Your uncle is well. God has healed him."

Then Juan asked, "What would you have me do? How do I prove to the bishop that you are the Virgin Mary?" The Lady said, "Juan, climb the hill. At the top, pick the roses you see growing."

Juan knew the hill very well. There were no flowers on the hill. Only cactus and bramble bushes grew on that bleak spot. Besides, it was December. Nevertheless, Juan did not delay. He wanted to be obedient. He climbed up the hill.

As Juan reached the top, he smelled a sweet aroma, then saw beautiful Castilian roses growing. Juan picked them quickly. The Blessed Virgin took the roses from him and put them in Juan's cape, called a tilma. She folded the tilma to cover the roses, and said, "This is the proof the bishop wants. Go and show him the roses. He will believe you."

Again at the bishop's house, the guards made Juan wait. Juan said, "I must see the bishop. I have a special gift for him." Finally, the guards allowed Juan to enter.

"Bishop Zumarraga, the Lady sent me. I have the proof you wanted," Juan said. He opened the tilma, and the roses fell onto the floor.

Our Lady of Guadalupe

The bishop hardly noticed the roses because he was looking in astonishment at Juan's tilma. On the tilma was a beautiful portrait of the Mother of God. She was dressed as an Indian princess. Her black hair was partly covered by a beautiful blue-green mantle. The colors of the portrait were brilliant and glowing. The picture of the Mother of God seemed to light up the room!

The bishop instantly fell on his knees. "Virgin Mary, Mother of God, forgive me! I doubted your messenger," the bishop said. "I will do as you ask. I will build a church on that hill in your honor."

Juan hurried home to see his uncle. Juan knew his uncle would be well. His uncle ran to the door. He told Juan a beautiful Lady had visited. "She cured me," the uncle said. "And the Lady said to me: 'I am Holy Mary, Virgin of Guadalupe.'"

Our Lady of Guadalupe

The Faith spreads in Mexico

Our Lady united the Indian and Spanish people. They spread the Faith throughout Mexico. Two hundred thousand Indians converted shortly after the miracle with Juan Diego! Less than ten years after the miracle, nearly all of Mexico was Catholic. The Mexican people built a beautiful church on the hill where Juan Diego saw and talked with Mary, the Mother of Jesus.

Our Lady kept her promise. She has spiritually protected Mexico. She has given the Mexican people spiritual strength. The Mexicans have endured anti-Catholic governments, poverty, and persecution. In spite of serious troubles, their faith in Jesus and His Church has remained strong.

Juan Diego's tilma is preserved by God even today. Four hundred years later, it has not fallen apart or decayed. It can be seen today in a new basilica in Mexico City.

The Basilica of Our Lady of Guadalupe. The old basilica is on the left; the new is on the right.

An American reporter asked a poor Mexican boy, "Shouldn't the Church sell the valuable things in Our Lady of Guadalupe Basilica? Shouldn't they use the money to feed the poor?"

The boy answered, "If they sell those beautiful things, we will have food only for a short time. The magnificent church has inspired us for four hundred years. We are proud of our faith in Our Lady. The Church feeds our souls forever. This is much better."

In 1921, enemies of the Faith exploded a bomb in the basilica. They hoped to destroy Juan Diego's tilma. The explosion shook the basilica. Yet, no one in the crowded basilica was hurt. The heavy metal crucifix was mangled. The bomb nearly destroyed the wall near the tilma. Miraculously, the tilma was unharmed.

The twisted cross was placed in a special chapel. The people still gather there to pray for those who persecute them.

In July, 2002, Pope John Paul II proclaimed Juan Diego a saint. His feast day is December 9.

St. Juan Diego, pray for us.

Our Lady of Guadalupe, pray for us.

Do You Remember?

1. Who discovered the Pacific Ocean? _____

2. Who conquered the Aztecs? _____

3. Who was the beautiful Lady Juan Diego saw? _____

_____

Map Study

1. Look at a map of Mexico. Find Mexico City. Is it north or south of the

   equator? _____

2. Find the Isthmus of Panama near Panama City. What direction is it from

   Mexico City?_____

3. Balboa crossed the Isthmus of Panama from the Atlantic Ocean to the

   Pacific Ocean. In what direction did he travel? _____

Chapter 4

The Conversion of South America

Words to Remember

hostile: very unfriendly

Jesuits: religious order founded by St. Ignatius Loyola

Dominicans: religious order founded by St. Dominic

Calvinists: members of a Protestant church that followed John Calvin

canonize: to declare a person to be a saint of the Catholic Church

Vespers: special evening prayers

Places to Remember

Florida: state in southeastern United States

St. Augustine: oldest city in U.S., located in northeastern Florida

Panama: narrow land area connecting North and South America

Peru: country in South America on the Pacific Ocean

Lima: city in Peru

People to Remember

Juan Ponce de Leon: explored Florida

Francisco de Coronado: explored the southwestern United States

Hernando de Soto: discovered and explored the Mississippi River

Francisco Pizarro: conquered Peru

Hernando de Soto explores the Mississippi River.

Early Spanish explorers

The Spanish sent explorers and missionaries in every direction from Mexico. They went north into what is now the United States. Juan Ponce de Leon explored Florida in 1513. Francisco de Coronado explored the southwestern United States from Arizona to Kansas between 1540 and 1542. Hernando de Soto explored the lower Mississippi River area in 1541. In 1565, Spanish settlers established the city of Saint Augustine in Florida. Saint Augustine is the oldest city in the United States.

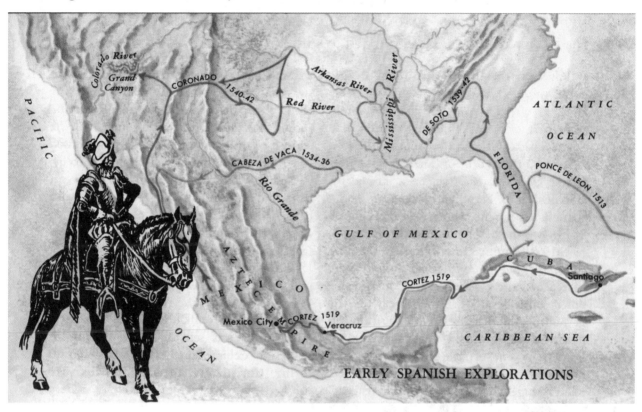

EARLY SPANISH EXPLORATIONS

The Indians in the southern part of North America were simpler and more friendly than the Aztecs. Many were converted by the Spanish priests who came with the Spanish explorers.

The Spanish went south into Central and South America. In Central America, they went into Cartagena on the Caribbean Sea. In South America, they went into Peru on the Pacific Ocean. The Indians in these areas had highly developed cultures. They spoke in simple but different languages.

Some Spanish soldiers were greedy and cruel. This gave a bad example to the Indians. However, the Spanish priests were kind and loving to the Indians.

The missionary priests came with the Spanish explorers. Sometimes the Indians would not listen to the Christian message because of the bad example of the Spanish soldiers. The Indians had to be shown how true Christians live. God sent three saints to the Indians to give them great examples of Christian virtues.

St. Peter Claver: The Apostle of the Slaves

Good men and bad men had arrived in the New World. Some had come seeking gold. Others had come seeking glory. Priests had come to seek the salvation of souls. In 1610, one of the greatest saints in the entire history of the Church arrived in the New World.

In 1605, at the age of twenty-five, Peter Claver entered a Jesuit college to study to become a priest. One of the workers at the college was a holy man named Alphonsus Rodriguez. In a vision, God showed him the great future mission of his young friend Peter. Alphonsus told Peter to go to South America. Peter obeyed. In 1610, Peter landed at Cartagena in New Granada. He continued to study to be a priest. In 1616, he was ordained.

In 1610, Cartagena was the center of the slave trade in South America. The Spanish colonists justified slavery by saying that the men and women they bought were already slaves in a pagan land. The colonists said that by bringing the slaves from Africa to a

Christian land they could be converted. Yet no one had tried to convert them. The Africans did not speak Spanish. Most of them were sick and starving. Many were dying.

The Church had tried to stop slavery. Sadly, the Church cannot abolish all sins. It was not able to stop slavery. The missionaries could not stop slavery. They could only ease it. No one worked harder to ease it than Peter Claver.

In 1622, Peter Claver began a holy work like none the world had ever seen. From this moment on, his life stands as an example of heroic charity. He found some Africans who spoke Spanish and also knew one or more of the African languages. They acted as his interpreters.

Every month when slave ships arrived, Peter Claver went out to meet them. He took food and water. The Africans were cooped up in the ship's hold. They arrived scared and badly treated. Peter went to each and showed them kindness. He cared for their wounds and sores. He made them understand that he was there to help them. Peter showed them pictures of Jesus and Mary. He showed them pictures of bishops rejoicing at the baptism of black men and women. Thus, he won their good will.

St. Peter baptized the slaves who were dying. Those who were not dying, he taught for several days. When they had learn a little of the catechism and the prayers, he had them say an Act of Contrition. Then he baptized them. During the course of his apostolate he baptized over 300,000 Africans. This was one-third of all the slaves brought into Spanish South America during this time.

St. Peter did not desert the slaves after they were baptized. He stayed in contact with them even after they were sold. He heard thousands of their confessions every year.

St. Peter Claver died September 8, 1654. Pope Leo XIII canonized him in 1888, and made him patron and protector of the black people. Pope Leo noted few saints have ever matched Peter Claver in holiness.

St. Martin de Porres

Across the continent of South America, Francisco Pizarro had conquered the Inca Indians in Peru in 1533. He had founded the city of Lima in Peru. In that city in the late 1500s, two people were born: Martin de Porres and Rose of Lima. The example of their lives would help the Spanish, Indians, blacks, and people of mixed blood to come to God's Church.

Saint Martin de Porres was one of two children born to a Spanish soldier and a freed black slave from Panama. Martin's father deserted his family when Martin was just a small boy.

Martin's family was very poor after his father left. His mother worked hard to raise her two children. She taught her strong Catholic faith to her children. She told her children, "God loves us all. We must help each other to reach Heaven."

Martin's mother and her children went to Mass daily. Their home was poor but happy. One day Martin said, "Mother, I want to serve God. I don't have an education so I cannot become a priest. Though I know I am not worthy, I would like to try to become a Dominican Brother." (Brothers are men who are religious, and do good works, but cannot say Mass and hear confessions like priests.) Martin's decision made his mother very happy.

Martin entered the Priory of the Holy Rosary. Here he prayed and did penance for the sins of all people. He worked very hard. He did many jobs. He was a barber, a medical helper, a wardrobe keeper, and a handyman.

His Dominican brothers would say, "Any one of these jobs would be more than enough for one man. Martin does them all. And he does them so well."

Martin did still more. He went out into the city to help others. He set up a hospital for the poor. He founded an orphanage for abandoned children. Brother Martin went to the docks to meet the slave ships. He took food, blankets, and clothes for the slaves. Upon seeing Martin, people would say, "Martin seems to be everywhere."

Brother Martin was put in charge of the priory's funds. He never hesitated to go into the streets and beg from the soldiers and wealthy Spanish. He would say, "Please help us. We need your money to help the poor. God bless you."

People knew Brother Martin would use their donations well. He would care for the priory. He would feed and clothe the poor of the city. On one occasion, the priory needed money to pay a bill. Martin offered himself as a slave. The man who was collecting the debt was impressed by Martin's humility. He said, "I couldn't do that, Brother Martin. I will tear up the bill if you will pray for me."

Brother Martin's good example converted many. He died on November 3, 1639. His life, spent in the faithful service of God, was very fruitful. In 1962, the Church canonized him. He is now Saint Martin de Porres.

Lima Cathedral

St. Rose of Lima

One of Martin's friends in the city of Lima, Peru, was St. Rose of Lima. Rose was born into a wealthy Spanish family in 1586. She was a beautiful child with such a pink skin that she was called Rose by her family. At an early age, she developed a strong prayer life. Rose would say, "Let me go to daily Mass with you, Mother."

Rose told her friend Brother Martin de Porres, "After Mass, I love to go to Vespers and Benediction at church." He replied, "That is very good, Rose."

One day her father said, "I made some bad investments. I lost most of the family money." Rose replied, "I can help. I can sew and embroider." So Rose began making fancy dresses for the wealthy Spanish ladies. In those days, all of the sewing was done by hand since sewing machines had not yet been invented.

Rose's father wanted her to marry a wealthy ship owner. Rose did not like to disobey but she knew that this was not what God wanted her to do. Rose said, "Please, Father, don't make me marry. I want to spend my life in prayer. I want to give my life to God." Her father answered, "If that is what you truly want, Rose, I won't stop you."

Rose joined the Third Order of the Dominicans. She was not a nun, but every day she prayed and did penance for the people of Lima. She told her mother, "I am most happy in the presence of the Blessed Sacrament." Everyone knew this. People would say, "When Rose receives Communion, the glow of her face could light up the church." Everyone loved and respected young Rose.

On July 17, 1615, a pirate ship attacked Lima. "Fire on the city!" the pirate captain cried out. The sailors followed their captain's orders. The cannons pointed toward the city of Lima and roared out with big gun blasts and dark smoke.

The people ran to Rose. They said, "The pirates are destroying our churches. What can we do?" Rose replied, "Follow me. We will defend our churches. We will pray that God will stop them."

They followed Rose to the nearest church to pray. The cannons fired for hours. There was great damage to the city. "Will the attack never stop?" people asked. They prayed with Rose all night.

St. Rose of Lima

Suddenly Rose sprang up and ran to the tabernacle. "They will have to kill me before they desecrate Our Lord in the Blessed Sacrament," she said. The people cried, "They will have to kill us, too." They surrounded the tabernacle.

At that moment, the guns stopped firing. One of the sailors cried, "What is wrong with the captain?" An officer answered, "He had a strange attack. He fell unconscious. Perhaps God is unhappy with us for trying to destroy the churches. Let's get out of here."

The pirate ship finally sailed out of Lima harbor. The city was saved.

Rose lived for two more years after the pirates left. She suffered a long and painful illness. Rose offered all her suffering for the poor people of Lima. Her good example brought many people into the Catholic Church.

Rose died on August 24, 1617. She was so loved that the whole city attended her funeral. She was canonized by Pope Clement X in 1671. She was the first canonized saint born in the Americas.

Christ in the Blessed Sacrament, we adore You.

Do You Remember?

1. Who conquered Peru? _____

2. Where did Ponce de Leon explore? _____

3. What is the oldest city in the United States? _____

4. Name three saints from South America.

_____

_____

_____

Map Study Skills

1. On a map of the United States, find Florida where Ponce de Leon explored.

2. Find one of the states Coronado explored.

3. On a globe or atlas, locate South America. Locate Colombia.

4. Find the city of Lima in Peru.

Chapter 5

The French Contribution

Words to Remember

Blackrobes: name that the Indians called the Catholic priests

gauntlet: a punishment in which a man was forced to run between two lines of men who hit him with sticks

beatified: declared blessed by the Church, the second of three steps towards being declared a saint

tomahawk: a small ax used as a weapon by Indians

Places to Remember

Saint Lawrence River: river between Canada and the eastern U.S.

Albany (Fort Orange): the capital city of New York State

Canada: the country to the north of the U.S.

France: large country in western Europe

Montreal: city in eastern Canada

People to Remember

Giovanni Verrazano: explored for France; sailed into New York harbor

Jacques Cartier: French explorer who discovered St. Lawrence River

Samuel de Champlain: the French founder of Canada

St. Isaac Jogues: one of the eight North American martyrs

St. Kateri Tekakwitha: Mohawk Indian girl; converted to the Faith

Shrine of the North American Martyrs in Auriesville, New York.

The French explore North America

In 1524, King Francis I of France sent Giovanni Verrazano to explore the New World. Giovanni Verrazano was the first European to sail into the New York harbor. He also sailed up the Atlantic coast as far north as Newfoundland.

When Verrazano returned to France, he gave a report of his travels to the king. Verrazano had not been impressed with the New World. As a result, the king did not send another ship to the New World for ten more years. Then the king sent Jacques Cartier to the New World. Cartier sailed north of the New York Harbor, and discovered the St. Lawrence River.

Cartier discovers the St. Lawrence River.

The French settle North America

When the Catholic people in France heard about America, French fishermen and trappers followed Cartier and the other explorers to North America. French families were interested in a peaceful location without the continuous warfare by France in Europe. This was the beginning of colonization, or settlements, by French families in North America.

Champlain, the founder of Canada

Many French went to North America to convert the Indians to the Catholic Faith as well as to trade with them for animal furs. Samuel de Champlain, one of the first French colonists, is called the Founder of Canada. He believed it was better to convert one Indian than to conquer an empire.

In 1615, Samuel de Champlain brought priests to Canada to teach the Indians the Catholic Faith. Because more help was needed, in 1625, French Jesuit priests arrived in Canada. The Jesuits founded a mission at Huronia. Many of the Huron Indians became Catholics.

Samuel de Champlain

The "Blackrobes"

The Iroquois, however, a warlike nation of Indians, attacked the Jesuit mission and destroyed it. The French king sent French soldiers to help the priests. The French soldiers burned the Indian villages of those who attacked the priests. After that, the Mohawks, one of the five tribes of the Iroquois, agreed to allow the missionaries to teach in all their Indian villages. The Indians called the priests "Blackrobes" because they wore long black cassocks.

For some years, the Blackrobes worked in peace. This did not last long, however. In 1642, the Iroquois attacked a missionary village at Montreal, killing priests and the Indians who had converted.

Father Isaac Jogues is captured

One day, Father Isaac Jogues, two lay missionaries, William Coutoure and René Goupil, as well as two leading Christian Hurons, and other Huron Indians were out gathering supplies. On the way back, Mohawks attacked them. Father Jogues and William Coutoure escaped. They saw René Goupil and several of the Huron converts captured. Father Jogues said, "I cannot leave these poor souls. I must give myself up to the Indians." Coutoure did not want Father Jogues to be alone. So the two holy men surrendered to the Indians to be near their Indian converts.

It took the group almost thirteen days to reach the main Mohawk Indian camp. On the way, the three missionaries were forced to run the gauntlet. That meant that they were hit with sticks by the Indians as they were forced to run between two lines of men.

The Indians and the Frenchmen finally arrived at the Mohawk camp. The Indians hit them again with sticks and pulled their hair out. They cut off Father Isaac Jogues' thumbs and forefingers as they wanted to stop him from holding up the Body of Jesus at Mass.

Isaac Jogues preaches to the Indians.

The brave missionaries still helped the Indian converts who were captured. They even talked to some of their Indian guards about Jesus Christ.

William Coutoure eventually escaped from the Indians. Rene Goupil was killed at Auriesville, New York.

Father Isaac Jogues spent thirteen months as a captive of the Indians. They forced him to be their slave. He was forced, as weak as he was, to haul water and wood. He did all the things he was ordered to do, offering up his sufferings for the salvation of the Indians.

At night, Father Isaac Jogues helped the Huron Catholics who were also captives. The good priest was able to baptize seventy Indians while he was a prisoner. Some of these converts died as martyrs at the hands of their captors.

Father Jogues escapes

The Indians moved from place to place. Finally, they arrived at Fort Orange, the Dutch area that is now Albany, New York. Father Isaac Jogues decided to try to escape and he succeeded.

The Dutch, though they were Protestant, hid Father Jogues from the Indians. They were shocked when they looked at his tortured body. They gave him clothes to replace the skins he was wearing. They helped him escape on a boat that went down the Hudson River to New Amsterdam, later called New York City.

Father Isaac Jogues was welcomed into the home of the New Amsterdam governor. A Protestant minister who was there was horrified at the sight of the priest's hands. The minister fell on his knees. He asked Father Isaac Jogues to bless him.

Pope Urban VIII gave Father Jogues permission to offer the Mass using the fingers that were left. The pope said, "It would be unjust if a martyr of Christ could not offer the Holy Sacrifice of the Mass."

Father Jogues rested and lived in a Jesuit house near Paris. It took him almost a year to recover his strength. Father Jogues then asked permission to return to Canada. The superior of the Order granted this request.

John Lalande, Isaac Jogues, and Rene Goupil

Father Jogues returns to Canada

The Mohawk Indians had always been in his prayers. When Father Jogues arrived in Montreal, in Canada, he begged to be sent back to the Indian missions. He told his Jesuit superior, "I know the language. I know the culture. I am suited for the work."

The superior said, "I hesitate to send you back to the Indian missions. But I know that your heart is already there. You may leave tomorrow."

Father Jogues knew he was making his last sacrifice. Before he left Quebec, he told a friend, "I shall not return." What courage Father Jogues must have had. How unselfish he was!

In 1646, Father Jogues went to the village where he had been a slave. As he entered one of the houses, he was killed by a tomahawk. Father Jogues became a martyr for the Indians he so loved.

The North American Martyrs

Eight Catholic men were martyred in the area between Auriesville, New York, and Quebec, Canada. They are known as the North American Martyrs. There is a shrine to them in Auriesville, run by the Jesuits. Saints John de Brébeuf, Isaac Jogues, Anthony Daniel, Gabriel Lalemant, Charles Garnier, Noel Chabanel, René Goupil, and John Lalande were canonized in 1930. Their feast is observed on October 19 in both the United States and Canada.

Many Indians became Catholic and were martyred by other Indians for their conversions. Among the Indians who were converted by the Jesuits, several are known to have given their lives for the Faith. The good example of the Blackrobes converted many Indians. They inspired many Indians to give their lives for God.

Stephen Tegananokoa, a Huron convert, was captured and killed by the Cayuga Indians. As he lay dying, he said, "I willingly give my life for God who shed all His blood for me."

Margaret Garangouas, the daughter of an Iroquois chief, refused to give up her Catholic faith. She was killed by her fellow Indians. Her last words were, "Jesus, Mary, and Joseph."

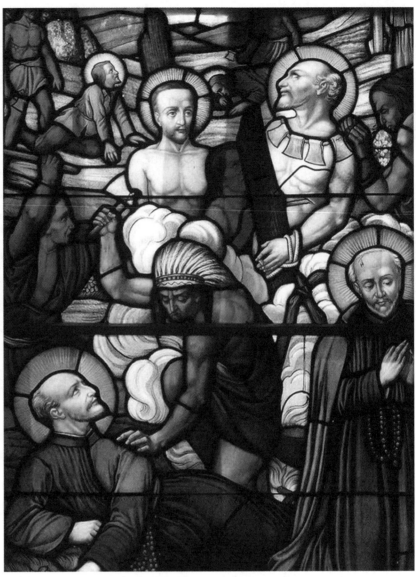

North American Martyrs

Saint Kateri Tekakwitha

The most famous of the Indian converts was St. Kateri Tekakwitha. She was born in the village where Father Isaac Jogues was martyred. Kateri was orphaned at four when her parents died of a disease. Kateri's face was disfigured as a result of her being sick with the disease. Her uncle, a fierce Mohawk chief, adopted her. He hated the Blackrobes, but he allowed them into the Indian village because of a treaty.

Kateri listened to the priests. She was converted on Easter Sunday in 1676. Kateri's uncle was furious. He was terribly cruel to her, and beat her, and would not give her enough food to stay healthy. His hatred grew every day.

Because she was in such danger from her uncle, a missionary priest, Father de Lamberville, helped her escape. He took her to a Catholic Mohawk village near

Montreal. There Kateri spent the rest of her life. She fasted, made sacrifices, and prayed for the conversion of the Mohawks.

After a long illness, Kateri died on April 17, 1680. Within moments after her death, her scarred face became clear and beautiful, as witnessed by two Jesuit priests and others in the room.

Kateri is known as the "Lily of the Mohawks." In 1980, she was beatified, called Blessed by the Church. Kateri Tekakwitha was canonized in 2012, the first North American Indian to be honored as a saint.

When you think about the North American Martyrs, think about the Catholic Indians as well as the Catholic priests who died to bring the Catholic faith to their beloved Indians.

North American Martyrs, pray for us.

Kateri Tekakwitha learns about the Faith.

Do You Remember?

1. Who was the first person to sail into the New York harbor?

   _____

2. Who discovered the St. Lawrence River? _____

3. Who is the Founder of Canada? _____

4. What did the Indians call the Jesuits? _____

5. Who is the "Lily of the Mohawks"?_____

   _____

Map Study Skills

1. Find Canada on a map of North America.

2. Find New York State. Try to locate Auriesville.

Chapter 6

Exploring the Mississippi

Words to Remember

calumet: peace pipe which guaranteed safe passage

ordination: religious ceremony that makes a man a priest

ransom: to free someone from captivity by paying the captors

Places to Remember

Mississippi River: major river which starts in the state of Minnesota and flows south into the Gulf of Mexico

Sault Ste. Marie: a Jesuit mission, now in northern Michigan

Five Great Lakes: Huron, Ontario, Michigan, Erie, Superior; the lakes form part of the boundary between the United States and Canada.

Allegheny Mountains: a mountain range in Pennsylvania

Atlantic Coast: the coastline on the East Coast of America

People to Remember

Louis Joliet: explored the Mississippi River

Jacques Marquette: Jesuit missionary who explored the Mississippi River

René de La Salle: French explorer who explored the Mississippi; claimed the area for France

Lydia Longley: first woman born in the English colonies to become a nun

Explorers carry their canoe across the river.

The English come to America

By 1607, about 100 men and boys had come to America from England and settled in Jamestown, Virginia. It was the first permanent English settlement in America. In 1620, English Pilgrims came and settled in Massachusetts. The English settlements were only on the Atlantic Coast. In the beginning, they did very little to explore west past the Allegheny Mountains.

Father Jacques Marquette

The French explorers, many of whom were Jesuit priests, had explored and claimed large parts of North America. Because the French and the American Indians were sometimes friendly, the missionaries could travel fairly safely. Unlike the English, the French traveled west of the Allegheny Mountains and the Mississippi River.

The French had explored large parts of North America.

Jacques Marquette was born in France in 1637. As a young man, he joined the Jesuits and became a priest. After his ordination, he asked his Jesuit superiors, "Please, may I go to the Indian missions in America? I wish to follow the example of Father Isaac Jogues."

The Father superior said, "You may go to America. You will go to Three Rivers Mission and learn the language and culture of the Indians."

After about a year of study at Three Rivers Mission, Father Marquette was sent to work with the Ottawa Indians at Sault Ste. Marie, in the state now known as Michigan, close to the Canadian border.

Louis Joliet

Father Jacques Marquette founded a mission for the Huron Indians in the area called St. Ignace, after St. Ignatius Loyola. It was here on December 8, 1672, that a canoe paddled into the mission area. Father Marquette asked, "Who has come?"

An old friend of Father Marquette, Louis Joliet, stepped out of the canoe. He was waving a paper. He said, "Father Marquette, I have news from Quebec. We have a commission from King Louis IX to explore the Great Waters. The King of France wants us to determine if the Great River flows westward to the Pacific Ocean. He wants to claim for France the land through which the river flows."

The two friends had much to discuss. Father Marquette said, "We will spend the winter here." Joliet replied, "Yes. We will need to gather supplies and canoes. We can get Frenchmen and friendly Indians to volunteer to help us."

"I will send an Indian to Quebec," Father Marquette said. "I will ask for a priest to come and replace me while I am gone."

Marquette and Joliet set off on their journey.

Marquette and Joliet explore the Mississippi River

The two friends, Marquette and Joliet, were ready to leave in the spring of 1673. They traveled across Lake Michigan, up the Fox River and into Lake Winnebago. Beyond was unexplored land to the Frenchmen. Friendly Miami Indians led the explorers overland to the Wisconsin River. Father Marquette and Joliet paddled down the Wisconsin River until they came to another river. The river was a mile wide!

This was the "Father of Waters" for which Marquette and Joliet had been looking. Now their exploration began. This river would one day be called the great Mississippi River.

Many rivers flow into the Mississippi River. Some of these are the Iowa, Missouri, Ohio, and Illinois Rivers. Along their travels on the river, the missionary-explorers stopped to rest several times.

The two explorers visited with the Indian chief of the Illinois tribe, who was a friend of the French. He gave Father Marquette and Louis Joliet a calumet, a peace pipe, to symbolize their friendship.

Father Marquette meets with the Indians.

As the missionaries traveled, they met many Indians. Father Marquette preached to them and many converted to belief in Jesus and His Church.

As the days and weeks passed, the Great River became wider and the days were hotter. Swarms of mosquitoes attacked them day and night. When Father Marquette and Joliet reached an Arkansas Indian village, they stopped to rest.

Father said, "Those Indians have Spanish guns. We must be near Spanish settlements." Joliet replied, "Then we are in danger. This is the lower end of the Mississippi River. If we go on, we will be captured by the Spanish."

Marquette and Joliet return to Quebec

The two men decided to go back to Quebec. They would report what they had found to the French king.

Friendly Indians guided them. The group went up the Illinois River. They traveled to a place near what would one day be the great city of Chicago on Lake Michigan. Marquette stopped in northern Michigan. Joliet journeyed on to Quebec.

Father Marquette and Louis Joliet had paddled 2,500 miles. They had found and mapped two routes to the Mississippi River. They had found that this river flowed through the heartland of what would one day be the United States of America. The Mississippi River ended much farther south in the Gulf of Mexico. The men claimed the land for France. Joliet took their reports back to Quebec.

Father Marquette had converted many Indians on his travels. However, he fell ill while preaching to the Illinois Indians. In the spring, he knew he was near death. He wanted to die in a mission with a priest.

Some of the Indians Father Marquette had converted carried him north. Sadly, before reaching the mission, he died in the wilderness. He was only thirty-seven years old. His body is buried at the mission at St. Ignace. He had given his life for the Indians he loved.

Later, Father Marquette's unselfish faith and courage were recognized in the United States by the state of Wisconsin. In 1896, a statue of Father Marquette was placed in the National Statuary Hall in Washington, D.C. His real monument, however, is made up of all the people he brought to Christ.

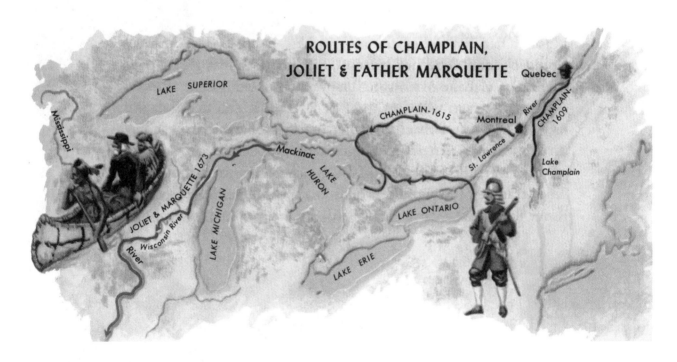

René de La Salle

In 1675, Rene de La Salle asked the French king for permission to explore the Mississippi River as well as the land nearby. La Salle said, "Your Majesty, I want to explore the western parts of the mission. If we can establish a settlement at the mouth of the Mississippi River, France will control the whole river."

The king answered, "You have my permission to explore. You may set up French forts. You may reinforce the French claims to all the land around the Mississippi River."

Rene de La Salle

La Salle returned to America and continued exploring American land. He claimed all the land along the Mississippi River for France. He knew that if France controlled the Mississippi River, the English would have to stay on the east coast. La Salle traveled down the Mississippi to its mouth where it empties into the Gulf of Mexico. He decided this would be a good place for a French settlement. However, La Salle died before it was settled.

Twelve years after La Salle's death, the first French settlers went to the land La Salle had explored, now called Louisiana. In 1718, La Salle's dream of a city at the mouth of the Mississippi came to pass. The city of New Orleans was founded.

Lydia Longley

The Catholic French, though they fought against the Protestant English, often helped individual Englishmen and their families. The Indians would take their English hostages to Montreal. There the French people would ransom English men, women, and children from the Indians.

In July of 1694, some Indians killed the mother, father, and five children of the English Longley family. Three other children were captured. One child died on the road. The Indians forced the boy, John, to live with them. The girl, Lydia, was ransomed by a rich French fur trader, Jacques Le Ber. Lydia was gravely ill. She was taken to his home and cared for by the Le Ber family.

Three years later, because of the family's good example and kindness, Lydia became a Catholic. Lydia wanted to give her life to God. The next year, she entered the Congregation of Notre Dame nuns. Lydia Longley was the first girl born in America to become a Catholic nun.

To the Frenchmen's credit, most of the English hostages who were ransomed by the French chose to remain in the French land of North America. The Protestant English were not persecuted as the Catholics were persecuted by the English Protestants. The good example of these hardworking, faithful French Catholics converted many of the English to the Catholic Faith.

Do You Remember?

1. Who explored the Mississippi River?

   _____ and _____

2. Who dreamed of a city at the mouth of the Mississippi?

   _____

3. Who was the first woman born in the United States to become a nun?

   _____

Map Study Skills

1. On a map of the United States, find the following:

   Wisconsin   Michigan   Illinois   Arkansas   Louisiana

2. Find the Mississippi River. Place your finger at the place where the river begins in the north. Trace it to its mouth in the south where the river ends.

La Salle views Niagara Falls.

Chapter 7

The English in America

Words to Remember

legislature: a group of people who are elected to make laws

House of Burgesses: the legislature of the English Colony of Virginia

Puritans: English Protestants who wanted religious freedom

Pilgrims: Protestants who came to America for religious freedom

Parliament: English legislature which makes laws

colonies: groups of people living in certain areas; they are like cities or states

Places to Remember

Jamestown: first permanent English settlement in America

Plymouth Rock: place where the Pilgrims landed in America

Maryland: first Catholic colony in America

Pennsylvania: first Quaker colony in America

People to Remember

George Calvert: First Lord Baltimore

Cecil Calvert: Second Lord Baltimore; founded Maryland colony

William Penn: Quaker who founded colony of Pennsylvania

Charles Carroll, senior: First Catholic attorney general of Maryland

King James I: English king who made George Calvert the first Lord Baltimore

King Charles I: English king who allowed the second Lord Baltimore to settle Maryland colony

King William of Orange: English king who made Maryland a royal colony

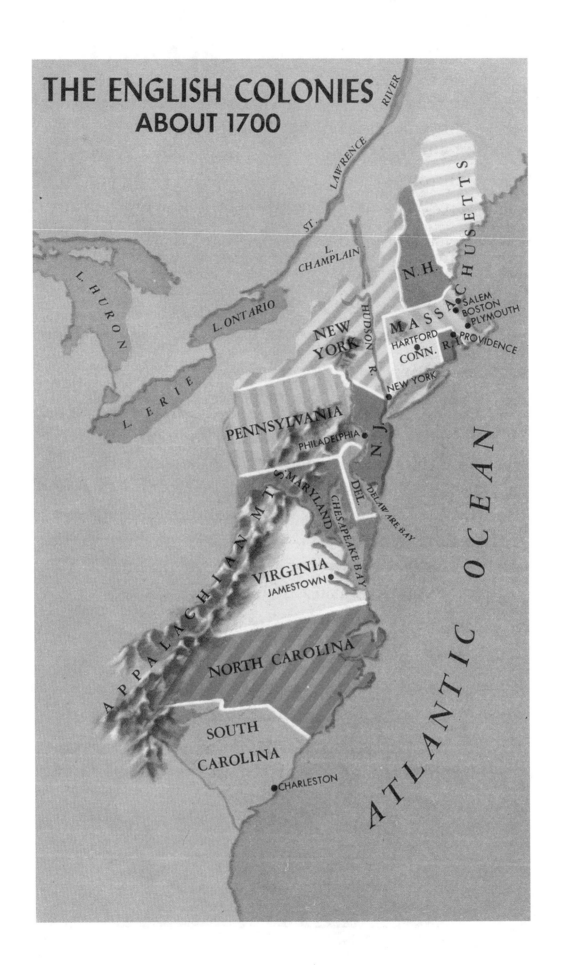

THE ENGLISH COLONIES
ABOUT 1700

L. HURON

L. ONTARIO

L. ERIE

ST. LAWRENCE RIVER

L. CHAMPLAIN

NEW YORK

N.H.

MASSACHUSETTS

SALEM
BOSTON
PLYMOUTH

HARTFORD
CONN.
R.I.
PROVIDENCE

NEW YORK

HUDSON R.

PENNSYLVANIA

PHILADELPHIA

N.J.

DEL.

DELAWARE BAY

APPALACHIAN MTS.

MARYLAND

CHESAPEAKE BAY

VIRGINIA
JAMESTOWN

NORTH CAROLINA

SOUTH CAROLINA

CHARLESTON

ATLANTIC OCEAN

We have learned about the Spanish Catholics in South America and in the southern and western part of the United States. We have learned about the French Catholics in Louisiana along the Mississippi River and in Canada. Now we will learn about the English, who were mainly Protestant.

The Virginia Colony

The English landed in Virginia in 1607. Jamestown was their first permanent settlement. In 1619, the House of Burgesses, where laws for the English colony were made, was founded. In that same year, a group of English women arrived in Virginia. They were prepared to settle down and raise families.

The Pilgrims

The English Pilgrims landed at Plymouth Rock, Massachusetts, in 1620. The Pilgrims were a group of Protestants who started their own religion in England. Henry VIII started his own religion and would not allow people in England to practice their own religion. He wanted everyone to belong to the Church of England, or they would be put in prison, or worse. So the Pilgrims escaped to America.

A Pilgrim Family

Maryland Colony allows freedom of religion

When different groups of people arrived in America, they would usually group together and call themselves a colony. Of the original thirteen colonies, only two had laws that gave everyone the right to practice their religion freely. One was Maryland, a Catholic colony that Lord Baltimore founded. The other was Pennsylvania, a Quaker colony William Penn founded. Quakers believe that all men are equal friends. They wrongly believe that no ministers or priests are needed.

The law in England at that time forced everyone to belong to the Church of England. The King of England had started the Church of England and he was the head of the church he started. Of course, Jesus made St. Peter the head of His Church.

George Calvert becomes a Catholic

George Calvert was born into a family that belonged to the Church of England. He was a friend of King James I. George Calvert was a Member of Parliament. Parliament was a part of the English government that made laws. He was a respected and important English citizen.

When Calvert studied the teachings of the Catholic Church, he realized it was the true Church of Jesus. He decided to become a Catholic. He knew his friends and the king would attack him for becoming a Catholic, since the king insisted everyone belong to the Church of England. Because of that, George Calvert was forced to give up all his government jobs.

Since George Calvert was a good friend of the king, he asked the king to give him some land in America. The king did and also gave Calvert the title "Lord Baltimore."

Cecil Calvert starts the Maryland colony

When George Calvert died, his son, Cecil, became the second Lord Baltimore. Cecil was also a Catholic. He asked the new king, King Charles I, to honor the agreement with his father. King Charles I gave Cecil Calvert permission to start a colony in America. It was called Maryland.

Cecil Calvert arranged for two small ships, the *Ark* and the *Dove*, to sail from England in 1633. Two priests sailed along with the colonists to Maryland. Some Protestants also went with the colonists. They all wanted to live in peace and not fight over religion. So when Lord Baltimore wrote the rules for the Maryland colony, he wrote that there would

The people in Maryland lived in peace.

be no state religion. All men would be able to practice their religion freely, whether they were Protestant or Catholic.

In 1649, the Maryland legislature, or Assembly, which made the laws for Maryland, passed Lord Cecil Baltimore's famous Toleration Act. The Toleration Act was the first law in America to allow the free practice of religion in a colony.

Today Americans are free to go to any church because the government does not require everyone to belong to one religion. Freedom of religion in the United States came about because of the principles of the Toleration Act of 1649, written by a Catholic for the Maryland colony.

Virginia attacks Maryland

The Maryland colony thrived. The only source of trouble came from some of the Protestants in the Virginia colony. William Claiborne, a Virginia officer, hated Catholics. He led many attacks into Maryland. During one attack, he captured Father White, one of the Jesuits in Maryland. He sent the priest back to England as a prisoner in chains. This was a truly disgraceful act in a new land to which people had fled for religious freedom. Some people wanted religious freedom only for themselves but not for others.

Priests are sent back to England in chains.

Claiborne also encouraged the Protestants in Virginia to move into Maryland. They began to become powerful there and worked to make Maryland a Protestant colony. By 1654, the Protestants gained control of the Maryland government. The Toleration Act of Maryland was thrown out. The Protestants began to persecute the Catholics. Catholics lost their jobs and other rights. Priests were forced to flee the Maryland colony in disguise.

By 1675, the third Lord Baltimore regained control of Maryland. He returned religious freedom to everyone. This lasted for about thirty-five years.

Maryland becomes a royal colony

Another very unfair action took place in Maryland in 1691. The Protestant English king, William of Orange, illegally took away Lord Baltimore's land and title. The English king made Maryland a royal English colony. He said that the Protestant Church of England was the official state church of Maryland.

Now Catholics were taxed to support the Protestant Church of England. The Mass was forbidden in Maryland. Priests were arrested for saying Mass. Catholics no longer had the right to vote.

In Maryland, under the Lords Baltimore, Catholics had prospered. They were among the richest families in the colony. They used their wealth to promote the Catholic Faith. They gave freedom to everyone. They did not persecute the Protestants or treat them unfairly.

Under Protestant rule, Catholic families like the Carrolls, the Darnells, the Brooks, and others used their large houses as places of worship. This was the only way Sunday Mass and the sacraments could be made available to the Catholics in Maryland. In their homes, Catholic parents secretly taught the Catholic Faith to their children. Families shared their religious books to help educate the children. Catholic families knew how to "homeschool" their children.

Wealthy Catholic families sent their children to Catholic high schools and colleges in France. With their early homeschooling and European college education, these Catholic children received a better education than most of the other children in America. When these Catholic children grew up, many of them returned to America. Some of them became important leaders in America.

The Carroll family

The leading Catholic family in Maryland of this time was the Carroll family of Carrollton. Charles Carroll, the Settler, was an Irish Catholic. He was a brilliant, well-educated man. He had been sent to France to study as a boy because of English persecution of Catholics.

The third Lord Baltimore had asked Charles Carroll to return to Maryland from France. Charles Carroll returned to Maryland and became an important lawyer and the first Attorney General of Maryland. The "pay" for this job was a large amount of land in Maryland. His land made Charles Carroll very wealthy. Charles loved Maryland and the Blessed Mother for whom some people believe the state was named. He raised a large Catholic family there.

Three grandsons of Charles Carroll became important in American history. His grandson, Charles, signed the Declaration of Independence. His grandson, Daniel, helped write the Constitution of the United States. Daniel's brother, John Carroll, was a priest who became the first Catholic bishop in the United States.

When we look at American history, we can be proud of Catholics. Catholics in Maryland began freedom of religion in America. While Catholics ruled the Maryland colony, there were never any laws against other religions. Despite all the persecutions, Catholics kept their Faith alive. Catholics played a large role in building the new nation of the United States of America.

God bless the United States of America.

Do You Remember?

1. Who was the first Lord Baltimore? _____

2. When did the English land in Virginia? _____

3. What was the name of the legislature of the English colony of Virginia?

   The _____ of _____

4. What was the name of the law of Maryland that gave religious freedom to all?

   _____

5. Who was the king who made Maryland a royal colony?

   _____

6. Where did the wealthy Catholics send their children to study?

   _____

7. Who was the first bishop in the U.S.? _____

Map Study Skills

On a map of the Unites States, find the following:

Virginia   Maryland   Pennsylvania   Massachusetts

The *Mayflower* lands at Plymouth Rock.

Chapter 8

Exploring the Southwest and California

 ## Words to Remember

padre: Spanish word for priest

diocese: the area under the care and responsibility of a bishop

architecture: a style of building

oratory: the art of public speaking

professor: teacher in a college or university

contribute: to give to a cause or fund

fame: a state of being well known by many people

peninsula: a body of land surrounded on three sides by water

 ## Places to Remember

Austria: country in central Europe

India: country in southern Asia

Mexico: country bordering the U.S. to the southwest

Baja California: peninsula extending from southern California; part of Mexico

Vera Cruz: city in Mexico

San Antonio: city in southern Texas

 ## People to Remember

Father Junipero Serra: Franciscan missionary priest to California

Father Antonio Margil: Franciscan missionary priest to Texas

Father Francisco Kino: Jesuit missionary to California & Arizona

Father Francisco Kino comes to America

Francisco Kino was born in the Tyrol Mountains in Austria in 1645. As a boy, he wanted to be like St. Francis Xavier. He wanted to be a Jesuit missionary to India. Francisco prayed and studied. When he grew up, he became a Jesuit priest. Then Father Kino asked his Jesuit superior, "May I please go to the missions in Asia?" His superior said, "You can go on the next ship."

Father Kino went to buy a ticket for the ship. The ship's captain said, "I am sorry; there is no more room on my ship."

It would be months before another ship sailed for Asia. The Jesuit superior asked, "Father Kino, would you go to Mexico, instead? We need priests there." Father Kino said, "Yes, I will go."

Father Kino explores and teaches

When Father Kino went to Mexico as a young priest, he learned to speak Spanish. He learned about farming and raising herds of cattle. After being in Mexico for a while, he wanted to visit the land to the north and do missionary work among the Indians of North America. Finally, he left Mexico City on horseback. He rode along the western coast and over to the area of Arizona.

Father Kino teaches the Indians to plant crops.

As Father Kino traveled, he made maps. The maps he drew of western Mexico and Arizona became famous. He drew the first map of the Baja Peninsula. People in Europe found Father Kino's maps very interesting, since they were unaware of the land in western Mexico.

Father Kino preached to all the Indians he met in Arizona and Mexico. Many of these Indians converted to the Catholic religion. He also taught the Indians how to plant crops and to raise cattle. He showed them how to irrigate (bring water into) the desert areas to raise crops, such as vegetables and fruit. He started a number of cattle ranches and taught Indians how to raise and handle cattle. He improved their way of life and taught them civilized behavior.

Father Kino's missions

The most famous of Father Kino's missions is San Xavier del Bac, located south of Tucson, Arizona. The mission buildings are the finest examples of Spanish architecture in the United States. Many times, the Pima Indians had to defend their San Xavier del Bac mission from the attacks of the Apache Indians.

San Xavier del Bac

The Apaches were the only Indian tribe to refuse to listen to Father Kino's preaching. They always rejected him and his Christian message of love and peace.

Father Kino traveled on horseback thirty or forty miles every day across the area of Baja California and Arizona. He was tireless in serving the Indians. The Indians called him "the Padre on Horseback" because he traveled so much.

Father Kino was still in the saddle at the age of sixty-six. One day, he was dedicating a new mission in Magdalena, Mexico. Father suddenly became very sick and died there on March 15, 1711.

Father Kino is responsible not only for the Catholic faith of the Indians in the southwest of North America but also for their fine farms and ranches. Father Kino was very dedicated to God and the Catholic Church. He was a great missionary and an American pioneer.

The people of Arizona chose to honor Father Kino. They placed a statue of him in the National Statuary Hall in Washington, D.C. Today you can see his statue there.

Father Antonio Margil

To the east of Father Kino's missions, across the Apache territory, was a priest named Father Antonio Margil. In the late 18th century, Father Margil converted many Indians in Texas to the Catholic Faith. Father Margil taught them how to provide for themselves. He also showed them how to live in well-planned towns.

Father Margil founded San Antonio de Bejar Mission. This mission is now better known as the Alamo. It is located in the present city of San Antonio. Father established a total of thirty-six missions for the Texas Indians.

The Alamo

One of his missions, San José de Aguajo, is one of the oldest surviving missions in the United States. The mission has a church and a large rectory. It had farms, ranches, and houses for the Indians who converted to the Catholic Church. The mission provided schools, a hospital, and defense against Apache attacks. The mission included a carpenter's shop where all the furniture was made. The Indians learned to weave cloth in a textile shop. The Indians built a tailor shop where they made clothing and blankets. They built a granary that held 4,000 bushels of corn. While the Franciscans ran the mission, it flourished. The Indians and the missionaries had homes and enough to eat.

Sadly, in 1793, evil men in the Spanish government took over the mission. The evil men allowed the Franciscan priests only to perform religious services but not help the Indians. In 1823, the anti-Catholic Mexican government forced the Franciscan priests to leave. The San José de Aguajo mission was almost destroyed.

When Texas became part of the United States, the mission became part of the diocese of San Antonio. It has since been restored to its original design.

Saint Junipero Serra comes to Mexico

Father Junipero Serra is probably the most famous of the Catholic missionaries in the United States. Junipero Serra was born in Spain in 1713. His father asked some Franciscan priests to teach his son. The boy was brilliant. At age sixteen, Junipero entered the Franciscan order. He was later ordained a priest.

Father Serra became famous in Spain for his wonderful speeches. He became a professor at the University in Palma. The students and teachers, as well as other educated people, respected and admired him.

After some years, Father Serra decided to give up his comfortable teaching job. He asked to be assigned to the missions in Mexico.

Father Serra's friends asked, "Why do you want to leave? Don't you like it here?" The priest said, "I have always wanted to be a missionary. I must go to the missions."

The Franciscan Superior sent him to Vera Cruz in Mexico. Father Serra was a short, somewhat heavy, round-faced, rosy-cheeked, middle-aged man when he arrived. He needed to learn to walk over the rough and hilly land of Mexico. He was often tired and out of breath.

Because of his fame for public speaking, he was asked to teach at San Fernando's College in Mexico City. Father Serra obeyed and taught for several years. Yet his true mission was still to come.

A Spanish officer asks Father Serra to go to California.

Father Serra goes to California

A Spanish officer in Mexico said to Father Serra, "California is very important. We need to have more Spanish missions there. Would you go?"

By then, Father Serra was in ill health. He had chronic lung trouble causing breathing problems. He had a painful ulcer on his leg. Yet he answered, "I will be God's Little Walker. Yes, I will go north to California, *amas a Dios*," which means "for the love of God."

Taking a few mules, cows, goats, and chickens, Father Serra walked from Mexico to California. He walked through a wilderness area with wild Indians. The Indians often fought bloody battles with each other. Many Indians were killed during these frequent fights. Father Serra hoped to bring the Catholic Faith, as well as order and peace to the Indians.

Father Serra's Mission in Carmel, California

Father Serra helps the Indians

When Father Serra reached California, he began to preach and convert the Indians. In doing so, he also taught them a better way to live. He turned battlefields into productive farmland.

Father Serra, the well-educated and cultured former Spanish university professor, loved the Indians. He would not let anyone hurt them. He once walked 2400 miles to Mexico City to talk to the Mexican officials. He told them, "Your governor is treating my Indians unjustly. He must be removed." Father Serra was then fifty-nine years old.

The official was so impressed, he said, "I will send a new governor back with you. I will tell the new governor to talk with you about the problems of the Indians."

Father Serra worked the rest of his life among the Indians in California. He became as well loved, respected, and famous among the Indians and the Spanish as he had been in the wealthy cultural society of Spain. After thirty-five years of missionary work in North America, Father Serra died at the Carmel Mission in California on August 28, 1784. You can visit his grave there today.

Father Serra's success

Nine of Father Serra's missions are now cities in California. These cities are: Carmel, San Diego, San Gabriel, Santa Clara, San Luis Obispo, Los Angeles, San Juan Capistrano, San José, and San Francisco.

After joining the United States, the people of California wanted to recognize Father Junipero Serra's contribution to their state. The people of California considered him the Founder of the state of California. They placed a statue of Father Serra in the National Statuary Hall in Washington, D. C.

PLACE	MISSION
CARMEL	SAN CARLOS
JOLON	SAN ANTONIO DE PADUA
LOMPOC	LA PURISIMA CONCEPCION
NILES	SAN JOSE
OCEANSIDE	SAN LUIS REY
SAN DIEGO	SAN DIEGO
SAN FERNANDO	SAN FERNANDO REY
SAN FRANCISCO	SAN FRANCISCO DE ASIS
SAN GABRIEL	SAN GABRIEL, ARCANGEL
SAN JUAN BAUTISTA	SAN JUAN BAUTISTA
SAN JUAN CAPISTRANO	SAN JUAN CAPISTRANO
SAN LUIS OBISPO	SAN LUIS OBISPO
SAN MIGUEL	SAN MIGUEL, ARCANGEL
SAN RAFAEL	SAN RAFAEL, ARCANGEL
SANTA BARBARA	SANTA BARBARA
SANTA CLARA	SANTA CLARA DE ASIS
SANTA CRUZ	SANTA CRUZ
SOLEDAD	SOLEDAD
SOLVANG	SANTA INEZ
SONOMA	SAN FRANCISCO SOLANO
VENTURA	SAN BUENAVENTURA

THE CALIFORNIA MISSIONS

The Catholic Church has recognized Father Serra's holiness and support for the American missions. On September 23, 2015, he was canonized. We can now pray to him as *Saint* Junipero Serra.

St. Junipero Serra, pray to God for us and for the American Indians.

Do You Remember?

1. Who drew the first map of the peninsula of Baja California?

   _____

2. Who was the founder of San Antonio de Bejar Mission?

   _____

3. Who founded many California missions?

   _____

4. What Indian tribe did the missionaries fail to convert?

   _____

5. Name the two missionaries in this chapter whose statues are in the National Statuary Hall.

   _____

   _____

Map Study Skills

1. On a map of North America, find the peninsula of Baja, California. It is south of Los Angeles and west of the Mexican mainland.

2. On a map of California, find the cities which began as missions of Father Serra.

3. Find Arizona and Texas on a map.

Chapter 9

The Carrolls in the War for Independence

Words to Remember

survivor: one who outlives others

inherit: to receive money, title, or property from a relative who has died

independence: freedom from being controlled by another

Places to Remember

New York City: a major city in New York State

Baltimore: a major city in the state of Maryland

Philadelphia: a major city in the state of Pennsylvania

Bardstown: one of the oldest cities in the state of Kentucky

People to Remember

Charles Carroll: only Catholic signer of the Declaration of Independence

Daniel Carroll: Catholic who helped write the U. S. Constitution

Archbishop John Carroll: first bishop in the United States

Benjamin Franklin: an American statesman who helped write and who signed the Declaration of Independence and the U.S. Constitution; obtained funds, soldiers, and supplies from France for the War for Independence

Signing the Declaration of Independence

Young Charles Carroll

Charles Carroll was born in Annapolis, Maryland, in 1737. He was named after his grandfather, Charles Carroll, Senior, the first attorney general of Maryland. Charles, Junior and two of his cousins, Daniel and John, were homeschooled in their early years. Later, they attended a school begun by the Jesuit Fathers.

The anti-Catholic law of Maryland at that time did not allow Catholic children to attend school. For a college education, the boys' parents smuggled them out of Maryland onto a ship to Europe. The three Carroll boys studied at St. Omer's College in France. Charles was a brilliant student. He returned to America when his father died. He inherited a great deal of land owned by his family in Carrollton, Maryland.

Charles Carroll inherited a great deal of land.

At that time, there were many people in the English colonies who wanted to be independent from England. Charles thought the same. God had given him a fine mind. He was a good writer and a good speaker. He was able to influence the other colonists about gaining independence.

Charles Carroll is elected to the Continental Congress

The people of Maryland respected and admired Charles Carroll. In fact, they respected him so much that the Protestants elected him to the Maryland colony's legislature, despite the fact that he could not vote.

In 1776, Charles was elected to the Continental Congress. The Continental Congress was a group of men who worked together to make things better for all the people in America. Charles promised to work for independence from England. He voted to separate Maryland from English rule.

Charles Carroll calls for American independence.

Charles Carroll was one of the signers of the Declaration of Independence. Charles added "of Carrollton" to his signature on the Declaration of Independence. He said, "Now King George will know exactly which Carroll signed here."

Charles also helped write the Maryland Constitution. Later, he became a United States Senator, representing Maryland in Congress. He urged the U.S. Congress to put the Capital of the United States along the Potomac River. He was the last surviving signer of the Declaration of Independence.

Just before his death in 1832, Charles Carroll said, "At ninety-five, I have had a rich, full life. I am most proud of the fact that I have always been faithful to the teachings of the Catholic Church."

Charles Carroll was the most outstanding Catholic layman of the time. He was a great American, too. He proved that a man could be a good Catholic and a good American citizen.

A statue of Charles Carroll now stands in the National Statuary Hall in Washington, D.C.

Daniel Carroll is elected to Congress

Daniel Carroll, a cousin of Charles Carroll, returned to America from Europe just as the War for Independence from England was about to start. This was the war which freed America from English rule. The thirteen American colonies became known as the United States of America.

After the War for Independence, Daniel Carroll was Maryland's representative to the Constitutional Convention. At that time, Congress elected the president. Daniel Carroll argued that the executive branch of government should be headed by the president. The people, not the Congress, should elect the president of the United States. Today, thanks to Daniel Carroll, the American people, not the Congress, elect the president of the United States.

Daniel's homeschooling by his parents and Catholic education in Europe helped him become a clear thinker, speaker, and writer. He said, "The United States Constitution is the best form of government ever offered to the world." This helped the people of Maryland understand and accept the new form of government.

Daniel picks the location for the nation's Capital

Daniel was one of three men chosen to pick the location for the nation's capital. His cousin, Charles Carroll, said, "Daniel, the Potomac River almost divides the nation in half, into the north and the south. We should set the capital in that area." Daniel Carroll agreed. Daniel was a generous man. He said, "I own a large farm on the border between Maryland and Virginia. I will donate the land to the new United States." Daniel Carroll's land became the home of America's capital, now called Washington, D.C. Daniel's land was used to build the Capitol Building where Congress meets.

The Capitol building in Washington, D.C.

Father John Carroll

Daniel Carroll's younger brother was John Carroll. While in school in Europe, John decided God was calling him to become a priest. In 1769, John was ordained to the holy priesthood. In 1774, he came back home to Maryland.

Catholics were not allowed to own church buildings in the anti-Catholic English colonies. Father John Carroll served as a priest at his mother's Manor House chapel. Father also traveled on horseback all over Maryland and northern Virginia to bring the sacraments to the Catholics living in the area.

In 1776, the Continental Congress chose some men to go to Canada. The Congress wanted Canada to help us fight for independence from England. Samuel Chase, Charles Carroll, and Benjamin Franklin were chosen for the mission. Benjamin Franklin said, "We will need to talk with the bishop of Montreal. We should take a priest with us."

Charles Carroll said, "My cousin, John, supports the War for Independence. He is a good priest and a fine speaker. He would be a great help to us."

Samuel Chase said, "I have heard Father John Carroll speak. You are right, Charles. He would be a great help to us in Canada."

Benjamin Franklin slapped his knee and said, "It is decided! John Carroll will go with us to Canada."

Benjamin Franklin was a key leader in the new American government. He came to know and like Father Carroll on their trip to Canada. They became good friends.

Bishop John Carroll

After the American War for Independence, American priests asked Pope Pius VI to ordain a bishop for the United States. Benjamin Franklin was in Europe near the Vatican at that time. The pope knew Benjamin Franklin was a key person in America's new government. The pope sent a messenger to Benjamin Franklin. He asked, "Mr. Franklin, do you know an American Catholic priest who would make a good bishop?"

Benjamin Franklin answered, "Yes, my friend, Father John Carroll of Maryland. He is good, kind, and smart. I recommend him."

Several years later, the pope appointed Father John Carroll as the first bishop of Baltimore. He served the Church as bishop for twenty-five years! Under his care, the Catholic Church in America grew quickly. The pope was so happy with his work that he was soon Archbishop Carroll.

Bishop John Carroll

When Archbishop John Carroll died in 1815, there were over 200,000 Catholics in America. The pope had created four new dioceses with bishops: Boston in the state of Massachusetts, New York in New York State, Philadelphia in Pennsylvania, and Bardstown in Kentucky.

Today the Catholic Church in the United States stands on the firm foundation Archbishop John Carroll built.

Immaculate Heart of Mary, protect the Church in the United States.

Do You Remember?

1. All three of the Carroll boys lived in which state?

2. What important document did Charles Carroll of Carrollton sign?

3. Who recommended Father John Carroll to the pope to become the first bishop of the United States?

4. On whose land was the Capitol building built?

Map Study Skills

1. Find Maryland on a map.
   In what direction do you travel from Maryland to go to Boston, New York, and Philadelphia?

2. Find Illinois and Indiana.
   In what direction do you travel to go to Maryland?

3. Find Kentucky.
   In what direction do you travel to go from Maryland to Kentucky?

Chapter 10

Catholics in the War for Independence

Words to Remember

taxation: money collected from citizens to support the government

representation: citizens elect other citizens to speak or act for them in running the government

tyranny: cruel and unjust government

immigrants: persons who leave their homeland to live in another country

chaplain: priest assigned to a school, hospital, military, or family

Places to Remember

Poland: Catholic country in central Europe

Savannah: city in the state of Georgia

Ireland: large Catholic island country next to England

Saratoga: city in western New York State

Vincennes: city in Indiana

West Point: United States military academy in New York State

People to Remember

John Barry: Irish immigrant; "Father of the American Navy"

Francesco Vigo: Italian immigrant; volunteered to spy for colonies

Thaddeus Kosciusko: Polish Catholic volunteer who fought for American freedom

Casimir Pulaski: Polish Catholic volunteer who fought for American freedom

Marquis de Lafayette: French volunteer; helped Washington's army

Count Francois de Grasse: French admiral; commanded French ships that helped America

Why the colonies wanted to be independent

"Taxation without representation is tyranny." This was what people in the thirteen original English colonies in America were saying. It is why they wanted to be free of England. But what do these words mean?

What is *taxation*? Taxation is a way for a government to collect money from its citizens. The government uses the money it collects to provide services for citizens, like building roads or paying for the police. It also uses the money to pay the army to defend the nation.

What is *representation*? Representation means that citizens elect other citizens to speak or act for them in the government. These other citizens run the government *in place of* the people who elected them. The English colonists in America had no representation in the English government, which was far away across the Atlantic Ocean.

What is *tyranny*? Tyranny is an unjust kind of government that does not give the people any say in how they are ruled. The people of the English colonies believed they were being governed by England with harsh laws and high taxes. They felt England was being unfair. Yet they could not change anything because England did not allow them to vote. The English government had all the power and control.

The colonists spoke out against tyranny.

England taxed the colonists for many things. The tax money went to England. The colonists resented this because they could not have a say, a vote, in how the money was going to be used. Most of the colonists wanted to be free of the English king, George III. Most colonists considered him a tyrant. Finally, most of the English colonists decided to fight against the English tyranny in the American War for Independence.

There were very few Catholics in the colonies at this time. Yet, Catholics played an important role in helping to free the colonies from the anti-Catholic English rule. The rulers of England persecuted Catholics. Many Catholics were happy to serve in George Washington's army.

Commodore John Barry

One of the most famous Catholic heroes in the War for Independence was Commodore John Barry. John Barry was born in Ireland. He came to Philadelphia, Pennsylvania, at age seventeen. Since Catholics were welcome in Pennsylvania, John made his home there. He worked on several merchant ships, hauling goods back and forth to America. Thirteen years later, he was captain of his own ship. He started his ship-day with a Bible reading to his crew.

By the time the War for Independence began, Captain John Barry was a rich man. Captain Barry gave up his wealth to help the cause of American freedom. The colonies had no navy and no ships. The American Congress asked Captain John Barry to equip a ship with his own money. Congress asked him to clear American waters of British ships. To do this, Captain John Barry supervised the building of a warship, the USS *Lexington*.

In Captain John Barry's very first battle, he captured the HMS *Edward*, an English warship. In fact, Captain Barry was successful in all his many battles at sea. President George Washington awarded the highest honors to Captain John Barry for his service, and put him in charge of the first warship of the United States Navy. This event took

John Barry prepares for battle.

place on George Washington's birthday, February 22, 1797. John Barry was given the title of Commodore. Later, he was in command of all American ships. Commodore John Barry is recognized as the "Father of the American Navy."

Francesco Vigo

Another Catholic immigrant, Francesco Vigo, came to the American colonies as a boy from Italy. He went into the fur trade. People used his furs for hats, coats, rugs, and blankets. He made a fortune selling furs. Vigo gave up his fortune to help in the American War for Independence.

At the beginning of the war, Francesco Vigo was working out of St. Louis. He agreed to spy for George Rogers Clark, an American military officer. The two men had a plan to capture the English-controlled city of Vincennes (in Indiana).

Disguised as a Cuban merchant, Francesco Vigo entered the English fort at Vincennes. He drew a map of the fort. He found out where the English kept the guns and ammunition. This information later helped George Rogers Clark capture the fort.

George Rogers Clark captures the English fort.

Francesco Vigo risked his life spying. He also loaned George Rogers Clark the money to pay for guns and food for the American soldiers.

With Father Pierre Gibault, Francesco Vigo spoke to some of the French Catholic settlers. The two convinced the French settlers to help the English colonies in the War for Independence.

After the Americans won their War of Independence, they had won a great area of land. The new nation controlled all the land from the Atlantic Ocean as far west as the Mississippi River. Vigo stayed and lived in Indian territory. However, he used all his money and influence to bring Catholic priests from Europe to serve the Catholic settlers.

Thaddeus Kosciusko

Thaddeus Kosciusko was a Polish Catholic. George Washington appointed this Polish volunteer to be an engineering officer in the army. Thaddeus Kosciusko was brilliant in designing and overseeing the building of protective forts for the soldiers. He built the fort at West Point on the Hudson River. He built other forts all along the Delaware River. The American victory at Saratoga was due to the fine fort he built.

Count Casimir Pulaski

Count Casimir Pulaski, another Polish Catholic volunteer, was appointed as a high ranking military officer, a Brigadier General, by George Washington. General Pulaski organized Polish immigrants into an infantry unit. They were responsible for the victory at the Battle of Brandywine Creek during the American War for Independence. After several other successful battles, General Pulaski was killed in the Battle of Savannah. He was thirty-four years old. Pulaski's last words were "Jesus, Mary, and Joseph."

Marquis de Lafayette

The Catholic French government was very kind to the colonists. The French contributed money, men, and ships to help the cause of American freedom. Several Frenchmen fought alongside the American colonists.

The Marquis (Mar key) de Lafayette is the best known of the Frenchmen who came to help the colonies. He was a brave young man. Lafayette became an important assistant to General Washington. Marquis de Lafayette kept his own chaplain with him. Lafayette wanted to make sure he would not die without the spiritual help of a priest.

Marquis de Lafayette

Count Jean de Rochambeau

Two other important Frenchmen helped the colonies. King Louis XVI of France sent 6,000 soldiers to America. The French soldiers were well-trained and ready to fight. They were a great help to the American general, George Washington, and played an important part in winning the War for Independence. The French soldiers were led by the Marshall of France, Count Jean de Rochambeau. A good practicing Catholic, Rochambeau had studied to be a priest.

Francois de Grasse

The French king also sent fifty-one ships to America. This was a very generous gift. The ships were commanded by Francois de Grasse. De Grasse was an admiral in the French navy. He brought the ships across the Atlantic Ocean to America.

Admiral de Grasse helped the most in the Battle of Yorktown. Led by de Grasse, the French ships forced

Count Jean de Rochambeau

the English fleet to retreat to New York. Because of this, the weapons and ammunition which the English General Cornwallis needed, never arrived to help the English. General George Washington defeated General Cornwallis at the Battle of Yorktown in 1781. Two years later, England and the United States signed a peace treaty in Paris. The treaty officially ended the War for Independence. The United States became a free and independent nation.

When word of the American victory at Yorktown reached Philadelphia, the Catholic French ambassador was overjoyed. He had mortgaged his own home to help the colonists pay for their war supplies.

The New Nation Gives Thanks

The French ambassador arranged for a Mass of Thanksgiving at St. Mary's Church in Philadelphia. Father John Carroll offered the Mass. The Mass ended with prayers for those who had died in the War for Independence. All over the United States, people joined the Catholics in giving thanks to God.

The Victory at Yorktown

Men from many nations fought and some died to win freedom and to establish the United States of America. Catholics certainly did their share to support, fight, and die for America's freedom.

George Washington, the first president of the new nation, wanted to say "Thank you" to the Catholics. President Washington made a small donation to help build the first Catholic church in Virginia, St. Mary's in Alexandria. George Washington told Father Carroll at the church's dedication, "I know how much we owe our American Catholics and the Catholic nation of France. Without their help, I doubt we would have won this war."

Father Carroll replied, "I hope and pray that all Americans recognize this. There is an anti-Catholic attitude in most of the states. Will that change?"

Father Carroll hoped that anti-Catholic attitudes would change. Jesus taught that we must always act with charity toward others, no matter what their personal opinion is about Catholics. We must stand up for what we know is right and true.

Do You Remember?

1. Who was the "Father of the American Navy"?

   _____

2. Who built the fort at West Point?

   _____

3. Who was a spy for the colonies?

   _____

4. Who commanded the ships that made the English retreat to New York?

   _____

5. Which Catholic country sent money, men, and ships to help the colonies?

   _____

Map Study Skills

1. Find Rhode Island on a map of the United States.

   In what direction do you travel to go to Pennsylvania from Rhode Island?

   _____

2. Find Indiana.

   In what direction do you travel to go to Pennsylvania from Indiana?

   _____

3. Find New York.

   In what direction do you travel to go to Virginia from New York?

   _____

Chapter 11

The Catholic Church Growing in the United States

Words to Remember

diplomat: a person chosen to represent his government to the governments of other nations

Constitution: national laws written by the founders of the United States

Places to Remember

Emmitsburg: town in Maryland; location of Mother Seton's Sisters of Charity

Boston: capital city of Massachusetts

People to Remember

Prince Demetrius Gallitzin: Russian immigrant who worked for the Catholic Church in Maryland, Virginia, and western Pennsylvania

St. Elizabeth Ann Seton: convert to the Catholic Church who founded the Sisters of Charity

Shrine of St. Elizabeth Ann Seton in Emmitsburg, Maryland

America Grows

Since 1776, the United States had its own government. Yet, the Congress, the lawmaking body, had no sure way to pay the nation's bills. So the Founding Fathers agreed to rewrite the basic laws of the nation. In 1787, the Congress wrote the Constitution of the United States. The new country and the Catholic Church then began to build and to grow.

Two important persons who helped with the growth of the Catholic Church in the eastern United States were Demetrius Gallitzin and Elizabeth Ann Seton. Both were converts to the Catholic Faith.

Demetrius Gallitzin becomes a Catholic

Demetrius Gallitzin was born in 1770 in the Netherlands in Europe. The Netherlands is also called Holland. The people who live there are called Dutch. The country is along the shore of the North Sea, to the north of Belgium and west of Germany. Demetrius Gallitzin's father was a Russian prince and diplomat, but he had no religious faith. Demetrius' mother was a baptized Catholic, but she did not practice her Catholic religion until much later in life. She did not teach her son anything about God. Demetrius was brought up as a pagan like his father.

IN 1772, TWO-YEAR-OLD PRINCE DEMETRIUS WAS MADE A CAPTAIN IN THE RUSSIAN ROYAL GUARDS BY THE EMPRESS CATHERINE II.

When Demetrius was a teen, he was sent away for military training. His father expected Demetrius to be a leader in the Russian army. However, something changed his life. When Demetrius was sixteen, his mother became seriously ill. She said to Demetrius, "Please get me a priest. I must go to confession. I have many years of sin to confess."

Demetrius' mother recovered and she began to practice her Catholic religion once again. She went to Mass. She prayed for her son. She prayed to St. Monica. St. Monica's son, St. Augustine, had converted to the Church after years because of his mother's prayers and good example. Finally, her prayers were answered. At age seventeen, Demetrius was baptized.

Demetrius Gallitzin comes to America

At the time, it was the custom for wealthy young men like Demetrius to travel to other countries for their education. In October, 1792, young Demetrius arrived in America. He immediately fell in love with the country. He said to himself, "This is a wonderful new land, this United States of America! But it has one big problem. There are so few priests here! People need help to care for their spiritual lives." Demetrius suddenly realized he wanted to help people to practice their Catholic Faith.

Demetrius went to Baltimore, Maryland, and offered his services to Bishop Carroll. The bishop said, "We do need priests very much. You can enter the seminary I started here and study to become a Catholic priest "

Father Demetrius Gallitzin

Demetrius changed his name to Smith. He kept the fact that he was a Russian prince a secret. In 1795, Bishop Carroll ordained him a priest. He was the first American-trained priest ordained by Bishop Carroll.

Father Smith began his work in Baltimore. Later, he worked for four years in Virginia and Maryland. Then the bishop transferred him to the wilderness that was western Pennsylvania. For forty-four years, Father Smith worked among the Catholic settlers over this large area in Pennsylvania.

Bishop Carroll ordained Demetrius a priest.

Father Smith traveled through snow and rain, in the heat of summer and in the cold of winter. He used his own money to build a mission center in Loretto, Pennsylvania. By the time he died, he had established ten churches and three monasteries in the Pennsylvania area.

Now there are four dioceses in the area in which he worked in Pennsylvania: Pittsburgh, Harrisburg, Greensburg, and Erie.

People who live in western Pennsylvania owe much to this humble, courageous man. He left the glamorous and elegant life in Europe to serve in an untamed wilderness. Demetrius Gallitzin, known as Father Smith, brought civilization to the American frontier of his day. In 1840, he died and left the world a better place than he found it.

Father Smith traveled in all sorts of weather.

Elizabeth Ann Bayley Seton

Around the same time that God blessed Demetrius with the gift of the Catholic Faith, Elizabeth Ann Bayley Seton also converted to the Catholic Church.

Elizabeth Bayley was born into a wealthy Protestant family in New York City. Though her parents were religious, they did not like Catholics. Elizabeth grew up reading the Bible.

When Elizabeth was older, she met the handsome and wealthy William Seton. They were married and had five children. However, William's shipping business began to fail. In addition, William became sick and could not recover from his illness. Finally, the doctor said, "You need a change of climate, William."

William told Elizabeth, "I have business partners in Italy. We can go there, Elizabeth, until I get better."

The long ocean voyage could be dangerous for young children. Elizabeth did not want to take all the children. We can take the oldest, Anna, with us. The others can stay with the family."

Young Elizabeth Bayley

Elizabeth Ann Seton learns about the Catholic Faith

After making arrangements, the three Setons made the long ocean trip to Italy. However, the change of climate did not help William recover from his illness. He died soon after they reached Italy.

Elizabeth and Anna were alone and unhappy in Italy. William's business partner, Mr. Filicchi, said, "Elizabeth, come and live with us for a while. We have room. You and Anna are welcome to stay with us as long as you are in Italy."

The Filicchi family members were good, practicing Catholics. They attended daily Mass. They said morning prayers, evening prayers, and the Rosary every day. Elizabeth was very impressed by their good example. The Catholic Faith reminded Elizabeth of all she had learned in her Bible studies.

Elizabeth and Anna stayed with the Filicchi family for about six months before returning home. She had to think about a way to support her children back in America. The Filicchis paid for her return trip to New York City.

The Cathedral in Livorno, Italy, where the Filicchis attended Mass. The original cathedral was destroyed during World War II. This cathedral is a copy of the original church.

After living with the Filicchi family and learning about the Catholic Faith, God blessed Elizabeth with the gift of faith. She learned that the Catholic Church is the true Church founded by Jesus Christ. From this, she knew that she should become a Catholic. It would not be easy, however. At that time, Catholics in New York City were disliked and often mistreated.

Elizabeth Ann Seton becomes a Catholic

All of Elizabeth's family and friends in New York were Protestants. She would be an outcast. Her family and friends would no longer want to help her.

Elizabeth prayed, "Dear God, please give me the courage to become a Catholic. Help me to take care of my children."

God answered both of Elizabeth's prayers. Mr. Filicchi returned to New York with her. He said to Elizabeth, "I have a friend. He is a priest. He runs a boarding school. I will pay for your boys to go to school there. That will help both you and the priest."

During Lent, Elizabeth started studying to become a Catholic. Her family was very upset. She told her family, "I must do what I know is right." Her brother said, "No one in the family will ever speak to you again." Despite the protests of her family, Elizabeth became a Catholic in March, 1805.

Elizabeth Ann Seton starts a school

Elizabeth was unhappy because of the unfriendliness of her friends and family toward her and toward other Catholics in New York. She finally decided to start teaching in a private school to support herself and her children.

One day, a priest from Baltimore, Maryland, came to New York. He met the young widow, Elizabeth Ann Bayley Seton. Father asked her, "Would you like to come to Baltimore to teach? There are more Catholics there and you can start a Catholic school."

Elizabeth was very happy with the idea. She said, "Yes, Father, I will come. I know my children will be happier there."

Elizabeth Ann Seton starts an order of nuns

In Baltimore, Elizabeth rented a house for herself and her children. It was both their home and a school. Later, other women came to help her teach. In 1806, she met Bishop Carroll. As she knelt before him, she told him, "Your Excellency, I would like to start a religious community of sisters."

"That would be wonderful! I need priests and sisters to serve the Catholics God entrusted to my care," the bishop said. "Why don't you use the rules of St. Vincent de Paul?"

Elizabeth answered, "Yes. We can dress in a simple black dress and the small black bonnet of a widow. It will be our habit."

So the Sisters of Charity began. Elizabeth became a nun. Her order of nuns grew as more and more women became Sisters of Charity. Many young Catholic women joined Elizabeth in teaching children. They started more schools. Before Mother Seton died, she and her nuns started schools and hospitals in Emmitsburg, Maryland, Boston, Philadelphia, and New York.

Mother Seton, as the other sisters called her, played a great part in the growth of the Catholic Church in America.

Mother Seton died in 1821. In 1975, Pope Paul VI declared that she was a saint. Elizabeth Ann Seton is the first person born in the United States to be canonized a saint. She is a patron saint of Catholic schools. There are many Catholic schools and even one home study school named in her honor.

Saint Elizabeth Ann Seton, pray for us.

Do You Remember?

1. Who was the Russian prince who became the first priest trained and ordained in the United States?_____

2. Who was Father Smith? _____

   _____

3. In which states did Father Smith work?_____

   _____

4. Where did Father Smith get the money for building his mission center?

   _____

5. Who was the first person born in the United States to be made a saint?

   _____

6. What community of sisters did she found? _____

Map Study Skills

1. Look at a map of the United States. Find the four cities where the Sisters of Charity had schools started by St. Elizabeth Ann Seton. Write the cities.

   _____ , _____

   _____ , and _____

2. Which of these cities is farthest north? _____

3. Which of these cities is farthest south? _____

Chapter 12

Three Bishops in a Young Church

Words to Remember

diocesan seat: the city where the bishop resides and the cathedral is located

frontier: an area of the wilderness in which people begin to settle; an area not settled enough to be called a town or city

seminary: a school where priests are educated and trained

Places to Remember

Bardstown: city in the state of Kentucky

Louisville: city in the state of Kentucky

Newark: city in the state of New Jersey

People to Remember

Benedict Flaget (Fla jay): first bishop of Bardstown, Kentucky

Stephen Badin: first priest ordained in the United States

Simon Bruté (Broo Tay′): first bishop of Vincennes, Indiana

John England: first bishop of Charleston, South Carolina

The pope creates four new dioceses

Bishop John Carroll told the pope that the Catholic Church in the United States was growing. The bishop suggested that four new dioceses be created. The pope agreed. He encouraged Bishop John Carroll to look for four priests who could be good bishops.

Father Stephen Badin and Father Benedict Flaget offered their services to Bishop Carroll in the new United States. Bishop Carroll sent Father Badin to the most western diocese, located in Bardstown, Kentucky. He sent Father Flaget to Vincennes, Indiana, in the central United States.

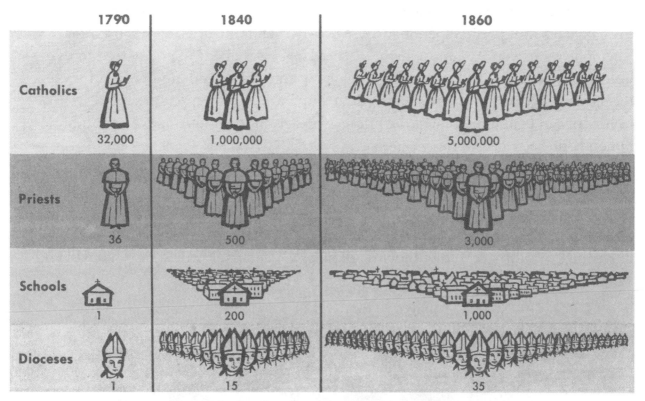

	1790	1840	1860
Catholics	32,000	1,000,000	5,000,000
Priests	36	500	3,000
Schools	1	200	1,000
Dioceses	1	15	35

The Catholic Church in the United States grew.

Father Stephen Badin

Stephen Badin was trained in France, but he was ordained in America by Bishop Carroll. Father Badin and Father Flaget had both come to America from France where they had escaped the cruel French Revolution. Evil men who hated the Church were ruling France. They killed priests and nuns. They closed monasteries and convents. Catholics in France were not allowed to attend Mass or receive the sacraments.

Father Stephen Badin worked in the Kentucky frontier. His central church was in Bardstown. He spent more time on horseback than on his feet. He was forced to travel long distances to find Catholic families and say Masses for them. He converted many people and brought the sacraments to the Catholic pioneers in the southwestern frontier. Everyone thought Father Badin would be the first bishop of Bardstown.

Father Flaget

The pope had other ideas. He wanted Father Flaget to be bishop of Bardstown. Father Flaget told Bishop Carroll, "I am not good enough to be a bishop. I hope my friend Father Badin will become the new bishop. He deserves the honor."

Bishop Carroll replied, "The pope wants you, Father Flaget. We must do what God and the pope want of us." Father Flaget was concerned because he truly believed he was not worthy to be a bishop. Father Flaget went back to France to talk to his religious superior about being a bishop.

Father Flaget asked his French superior to speak to the pope for him and ask the pope to change his mind. The superior answered, "My friend, the decision has been made. The pope wants you. You must serve." Father Flaget was obedient and agreed to be a bishop. While he was in France, Father Flaget went to his friends and begged for money for his new diocese in America. Father even convinced some French priests to go back to America to help him. One of the priests who agreed to go to America with him was Simon Bruté.

Bishop Flaget

When Father Flaget returned to America, he was consecrated the sixth United States bishop. His diocesan territory was huge, covering the area that later became the states of Kentucky, Tennessee, Ohio, Indiana, Illinois, Wisconsin, Minnesota, Arkansas, and Missouri!

Bishop Flaget did an amazing job. He traveled throughout his whole diocese every year. Everyone loved this humble bishop. It was obvious that the pope chose the right priest to be the bishop.

Bishop Flaget built many churches and schools. He brought more priests and religious from Europe to serve his people. He also created orders of American nuns.

The Catholic population in Bishop Flaget's care grew in number. The bishop requested the pope to make four additional dioceses out of the huge wilderness. The pope agreed. Everyone in these areas knew and respected Bishop Flaget.

Bishop Flaget established Saint Joseph's College and St. Mary's College Seminary. He also designed and supervised the building of the cathedral at Bardstown. However, Bishop Flaget realized that even though he loved Bardstown, the future population of Kentucky would be around the city of Louisville. He suggested to the pope that the diocesan seat be moved there. The pope agreed.

Bishop Flaget spent the last nine years of his life as Bishop of Louisville. Bishop Flaget died in 1850 at the age of eighty-seven. Bishop Flaget was a priest for sixty-two years. He was a bishop on the American frontier for forty of these years. All the Catholics on the frontier loved him.

Vincennes

One of the new dioceses created out of the Bardstown diocese was Vincennes, Indiana.

Bardstown Cathedral

Bishop Flaget told Father Simon Bruté, "The pope wants you as bishop of Vincennes. You will obey God and the pope. You will become the bishop of Vincennes."

Simon grows up in France

As a young boy, Simon Bruté had lived in France during the French Revolution. His mother, a devout Catholic, had hidden priests in their house to protect them from death at the hands of the evil men who ruled France. Simon's mother had put her son to work in the family printing shop. This protected him from being forced to join the army.

As a boy, Simon Bruté had smuggled Communion hosts into the French prison. This helped priests receive Jesus in the Blessed Sacrament one last time before being killed by the French government. Both Simon and his mother risked their lives many times to keep the Catholic Faith alive in France.

After the French Revolution ended, Simon became a college medical student. When some of his professors taught evil ideas, Simon stood up to them. Simon was responsible for good reforms in his medical school. When he graduated, everyone expected Simon to become a doctor. He surprised everyone and said that he would become a priest.

Father Simon Bruté

Since the seminaries and convents had been closed for ten years, there were few young priests in France. After Father Bruté was ordained, he was much in demand. The bishop of Rennes in France asked Father Bruté to teach at his seminary. Father Bruté became a teacher at the seminary.

When Father Flaget went to France to find priests to work in America, Father Simon Bruté agreed to leave his teaching job at the French seminary and go to America with him. As soon as their ship docked in Baltimore, Father Bruté went to see Archbishop Carroll.

Father Bruté told Archbishop Carroll, "I want to help build the Catholic Church in America. What can I do to help?"

The archbishop answered, "We need men with your training to teach in the seminary at Emmitsburg. Will you help train priests?"

The young immigrant priest said, "I will be happy to help. But I would like to study the Indian language. When I know this language, I would like to go west and work with the Indians."

For twelve years, Father Bruté taught at Mount Saint Mary's Seminary in Emmitsburg, Maryland. Father Bruté also became the chaplain for the Sisters of Charity, Mother Seton's new order of nuns. Father Bruté went to their convent to say Mass, to hear confessions, and to counsel the Sisters.

Bishop Bruté

Father Bruté was very happy in his work for God and the Church. Then, in 1834, the pope chose him to be the first bishop of Vincennes, Indiana. This would be a big change for Father Bruté. Both Bishop Flaget and Bishop Purcell traveled with their friend, Bishop Bruté, to Vincennes, Indiana.

In Indiana, crowds of people came out to greet the three bishops. The leader of the crowd was Francesco Vigo. He said, "I have worked and prayed for this day. How happy I am that we now have a bishop at Vincennes."

Bishop Flaget knew Francesco Vigo. The bishop exclaimed, "Francesco, you have always supported the Church. You helped me when I was a missionary here. I know you will help Bishop Bruté."

Francesco knelt and kissed the bishop's ring. The crowd cheered, "God bless our bishop, Bishop Bruté."

The people were very excited to welcome Bishop Bruté. There was much to do in the Indiana frontier. There were only three priests and Bishop Bruté to help serve Catholics in an area the size of the state of Indiana and part of Illinois.

Bishop Bruté and the Indians

Bishop Bruté traveled by horseback all over his diocese to see what was needed. One of his stops was at an Indian village. The Indian village was on the Saint Joseph's River near Lake Saint Mary.

Bishop Bruté baptized one hundred and twenty people and confirmed two hundred and fifty in both the town and the Indian village. It was the beginning of a great future for Catholics in Indiana.

The Indians of the village were very happy to see the bishop. The Indian chief said, "I will give you land for the Church to use as a school. I will give you six-hundred twenty-five acres of land." The bishop said, "Thank you for this great donation to the Church.

Someday there will be a great school here."

The bishop was very grateful and continued to thank the chief. The Indian village later became a town. Now it is called South Bend, Indiana. True to Bishop Bruté's prediction, the Indian village became the home of Notre Dame University, which in French means Our Lady's University. It is also the home of St. Mary's College.

Bishop Bruté's diocese grows

The rest of Bishop Bruté's life was spent traveling. He traveled by horseback around his huge diocese once every year. He went to Europe twice to find priests and nuns to come to America. He begged for money for his American mission territory. With the money, he built churches, schools, orphanages, and hospitals. Bishop Bruté wrote letters and even wrote books in defense of the Catholic Faith. These books were important since he could not see all the Catholics each week.

Bishop Bruté traveled by horseback around his huge diocese.

One of the local Protestant ministers challenged Bishop Bruté about his knowledge of the Bible. Bishop Bruté and the minister had a public debate. Bishop Bruté had been well educated at the French medical college and the French seminary. He spoke very well. Many of the Protestants in the crowd later converted to the Catholic Church. The debate gained Bishop Bruté great respect and a reputation for his knowledge of the Bible.

When Bishop Bruté died some years later, he was buried at the cathedral he had built in Vincennes, Indiana.

Bishop John England of Charleston

The Church grew quickly in the United States because of the hard work of men like Bishop Flaget, Bishop Bruté, and Bishop John England. In 1822, Bishop John England started the first Catholic newspaper in the United States to help new Catholics learn about the Church. The paper was called the *Catholic Miscellany*. He also became the first bishop of the Charleston diocese.

John England was born in County Cork, Ireland, in 1786. When he lived in Ireland, John helped the Irish people. When he moved to the United States, Bishop England continued to help the Irish struggling in a new land. He also supported the rights of African Americans.

Pope Pius VII appointed John the first bishop of the new diocese of Charleston in 1820. At the time of his

The old cathedral in Vincennes, Indiana

arrival, there were only two churches in the entire diocese. The diocese was spread over three states: North Carolina, South Carolina, and Georgia. During his time as bishop, he traveled all over the diocese meeting people and setting up new churches. He traveled to Europe many times to raise money for his diocese.

Not only was Bishop England a good bishop, he was also a good law maker. Congress invited him to discuss his ideas for new laws in South Carolina. Congress accepted the laws he suggested. On January 8, 1826, Bishop John England became the first Catholic priest to preach in the U.S. House of Representatives.

Bishop England worked so hard for his diocese that he finally became very weak. After one of his many trips to Europe, he died in 1842.

Jesus, Mary, and Joseph, help our bishops.

Do You Remember?

1. Who was the first bishop of Bardstown, Kentucky? _____

   _____

2. The diocesan seat was moved from Bardstown to what other

   city in Kentucky? _____

3. Who was the first bishop of Vincennes, Indiana? _____

   _____

4. Who was the first bishop of Charleston, South Carolina? _____

   _____

5. Who was the first priest to speak before the U.S. House of Representatives?

   _____

Map Study Skills

1. On a map, find the following:

   the state of Kentucky

   the state of Indiana

   South Bend, Indiana

2. On a map, find the following:

   Bardstown, Kentucky

   Louisville, Kentucky

   Vincennes, Indiana

Bishop John England

Chapter 13

Friends of the Indians

Words to Remember

nun: religious sister who lives in community in a convent

hardships: sufferings that are hard to bear

final vows: a promise made before God to be a nun for life

monastery: place where nuns or religious brothers live in a community

novitiate: place where girls train to be nuns

Places to Remember

St. Louis: city in the state of Missouri

Kansas: state in the midwestern United States

Utah: state in the western United States

Washington: state on the northwestern coast of the United States

People to Remember

Saint Rose Philippine Duchesne (Doo Shane): Sister of the Sacred Heart

Father Peter de Smet: Belgian Jesuit missionary to the Indians

Chief Sitting Bull: chief of the Sioux (soo) Indians

Saint Madeleine Sophie Barat: founder of the Society of the Sacred Heart

Catholic priests and nuns have worked among the Indians since the first French and Spanish explorers arrived in the Americas. Two of them, a nun and a priest, had a big effect on settling the midwest and the western United States. They are Saint Rose Philippine Duchesne and Father Peter de Smet.

Philippine Duchesne grows up in France

Philippine Duchesne was born in France in 1769. She was a very happy child. She loved to play with her brothers and sisters. As she grew up, she decided that she wanted to join a convent and become a Visitation nun. That way, she could dedicate her life to prayer and helping others.

St. Rose Philippine Duchesne

Her father, who was a lawyer and the mayor of their town, said, "I don't think that is wise. The way things are going in France, there may not be convents or monasteries in a few years. The rulers do not like Catholics. You would be better off getting married."

Philippine said, "Father, please let me go. I will not take final vows until you know whether or not the Visitation Convent will stay open. I want to go and serve God."

Her father answered, "I will talk to the Mother Superior of the convent."

Philippine's father went to visit the convent. He said to the Mother Superior, "I believe our French government will soon close all convents and monasteries. I think we will suffer a great deal. I don't want my daughter to take final vows until I am sure of what will happen."

The Mother Superior agreed that his daughter would not take final vows. Philippine entered the convent and took the name of Rose, after St. Rose of Lima, Peru. Philippine entered the convent of the Visitation nuns when she was eighteen years old. Unfortunately, her father was right. The French Revolution broke out in 1789. Two years later, the French government forced all the Catholic churches, convents, and monasteries to close. In fact, the Visitation Convent was turned into a prison for any who opposed the evil government. The French government killed thousands of Catholic priests, nuns, and lay people. Philippine was forced to return home. Her father's important position protected her from being captured.

For fifteen years, Philippine lived a quiet life of prayer, penance, and charity in her father's home. She started a secret Ladies of Mercy group. They did what they could to help prisoners and priests in hiding. Finally, after about ten years, the government changed.

Philippine then used her own family's money to buy and reopen the former Visitation Convent. After about three years, she met the saintly Mother Madeleine Sophie Barat. Madeleine Sophie Barat had recently started a new order of nuns called The Society of the Sacred Heart. Though Mother Barat was only 25 years old, Philippine instantly knew God wanted her to join the Society of the Sacred Heart. Philippine fell to her knees at meeting Mother Barat, and kissed her feet.

Mother Madeleine Sophie Barat

Philippine gave her convent to the Society of the Sacred Heart. She later took her final vows as a Sacred Heart nun. Mother Barat recognized the talents of Mother Duchesne, and assigned her to run the convent in Paris. Mother Rose Philippine Duchesne knew important people because of her influential and rich family.

Mother Duchesne comes to America

In 1804, Mother Duchesne heard a sermon from a priest who was a missionary in America. He spoke about the mission to the Indians. From that moment on, Mother Duchesne had a desire to go to America to serve the Indians. She began to offer her prayers and sacrifices for the Indians.

In 1817, the bishop of St. Louis, Missouri, went to France to beg for missionary sisters. He asked Mother Barat for a few nuns to help him. Mother Duchesne fell to her knees in front of Mother Barat. She begged to be allowed to do missionary work among the Indians. Mother Barat was stunned and silent. After some moments of silent prayer, Mother Barat said yes.

At last, in March of 1818, at age forty-nine, Mother Rose Philippine Duchesne was placed in charge of four other Sacred Heart nuns and sailed for America. They were bound for Saint Louis, Missouri, and then for the Indian missions in Kansas.

The bishop greeted them in Saint Louis. "Sisters, you cannot go to Kansas. It is too dangerous. I am sending you to St. Charles, Missouri, to start a school." Mother answered, "We will do as you say, Your Excellency. I pray that someday we will be able to work with the Indians."

Mother Duchesne works in America

Mother Duchesne and the four nuns opened the first free school west of the Mississippi. Many students joined the school, so it grew quickly. The next year, a group of families asked them to open a school in the Missouri Valley. It was a boarding school and a novitiate.

Mother Duchesne then opened an orphanage, an academy school, and a free school in St. Louis. The Sacred Heart Order and the schools did well despite many problems. Mother Barat was correct about Mother Duchesne's talents.

Mother Duchesne opened a free school.

Mother Duchesne works with the Indians

One day, one of the nuns asked Mother Duchesne, "Will we ever get permission to teach the Indians?"

Mother replied, "I hope and I pray that we will, some day soon."

In 1841, when Mother Duchesne was seventy-two years old, she finally received permission to teach the Indians in Kansas. She said, "Thank God! Our prayers are answered. But I am too old to learn the Indian language. I must teach them by kindness and charity."

When Mother Duchesne went to teach the Indians, she spent four hours in the morning and four hours at night in the chapel. She was praying that God would bless her work. She prayed to God to help her convert the Indians to the true Faith. Due to her many prayers in the chapel, the Indians called her, "The woman who always prays."

Mother Duchesne worked only one year among her beloved Indians. Her poor health and the hardships of life among the Indians caused her superiors to send her back to Saint Charles. She died there at the age of eighty-three.

Mother Duchesne worked only one year among her beloved Indians.

Saint Rose Philippine Duchesne

Those who knew Mother Rose Philippine Duchesne considered her to be a saint even while she was alive. Her life of humility, prayer, and service to others was clear to all. Father Peter de Smet knew her well. He said he never left her without the feeling that he had been talking to a saint.

In 1988, Pope John Paul II canonized Rose Philippine Duchesne. Her work among the Indians and the families of the settlers brought both hope and love to a rough pioneer society.

Saint Rose Philippine Duchesne, pray for us.

Father Peter de Smet comes to America

The Indians had another good friend at that time. His name was Father Peter de Smet. Peter was born in 1801 in Belgium, a country in Europe on the coast of the North Sea. As a little boy, Peter wanted to be a soldier. Later, he decided to go to a seminary to train for the priesthood.

A priest from Kentucky came to the Belgian seminary. He was asking for priests to go to the Indian missions in America. Peter de Smet and one other seminarian volunteered. They left on a ship for America shortly after that.

When the three men arrived in Baltimore, Maryland, the priest said, "Good-bye, I am leaving you with the Jesuit rector. I hope you will join me in the missions when you are ordained."

The three men entered the Jesuit seminary in Maryland. The next year, a new Jesuit seminary in Missouri was opened. Peter volunteered to go. He was finally ordained there in 1827.

Father Peter de Smet works with the Indians

Father Peter de Smet works with the Indians.

Father Peter de Smet wanted to start his work with the Indians. He said to his religious superior, "I have a strong desire to serve the Indians. Please give me a job in the West."

Just then, some Flathead Indians came into the superior's office. It was their fourth trip to Saint Louis to ask the bishop for a priest. The chief said, "Good Father, we need a Blackrobe to help us. We love God. We want the Mass and the sacrament of Penance."

The Indians inspired Father de Smet. He said, "Superior, let me go and serve this good tribe of people." The Superior gave his permission. In March of 1840, Father de Smet went on the first of many trips to the Rocky Mountains to serve the Indians.

Father Peter de Smet spent the rest of his life serving the Indians. He baptized thousands of Indian people. Three times he went to Europe to find more priests and nuns, and to raise money for his missions. Father de Smet brought the first nuns into the state of Washington to start schools. He never stopped working for the Indians.

Father de Smet was so loved by the Indians that he could go anywhere. He was the only white man allowed at the Indian meetings. He used this opportunity to preach and teach the Indians about Jesus.

Father de Smet works for peace

During the Civil War (or the War Between the States), Father de Smet acted on behalf of President Abraham Lincoln with the Indians. After the war, in 1868, the Sioux Nation declared war on the United States. They refused any talk of peace. Father de Smet was asked to go alone to Powder River, in Wyoming Territory, the Sioux Nation's home. Father was sixty-eight and in poor health. Yet, he put aside his own suffering and made the long journey to Wyoming. It took fifty days to reach the Indian camp. The Indian guide said, "Blackrobe, you have been good to the Indians. We trust you. No other white man could enter here and come out alive."

The leader of the Sioux was Chief Sitting Bull. Sitting Bull was at an Indian meeting when Father de Smet arrived. The priest entered the meeting lodge. Sitting Bull said, "The white men started the war. I am sorry so much blood has been shed. I hate the white men, but I trust you. We will listen to what you have to say."

The meeting lasted four hours. By the grace of God, Father de Smet convinced the Indians to talk to the United States government about peace.

Father de Smet went to his lodge to rest before the long trip back to Saint Louis. Suddenly, Indian women came into his lodge with their children and babies. They asked Father, "Blackrobe, please bless our children." Father de Smet's mission was a success.

Father Peter de Smet

Father de Smet becomes ill

After returning to Saint Louis, the elderly priest was exhausted. Fr. de Smet did not realize how sick he was. In May, 1873, Father de Smet died. When Peter de Smet was ordained as a priest, there were only 4,000 people in Saint Louis. When he died, there were 450,000 people. There was one church in St. Louis when he arrived. There were thirty-six churches when he died.

The Indians lost their best friend. He gave the Indians hope. Through the Catholic Church, he assured them of a better life in Heaven. No one could take this away from them. Father de Smet was truly a great Catholic missionary.

Do You Remember?

1. Where was Saint Rose Philippine Duchesne born?

   _____

2. With what community of Sisters did she take her final vows?

   _____

3. How old was she when she was finally allowed to work with the Indians?

   _____

4. What order of priests did Father de Smet join?

   _____

5. Who were the first Indians Father de Smet helped?

   _____

6. What Indian chief made peace with the United States government because of Father de Smet?

   _____

Map Study Skills

On a map, find the following:

St. Louis, Missouri   St. Charles, Missouri

Kansas   Washington   Wyoming

Chapter 14

Oregon Territory

Words to Remember

oath of allegiance: promise of loyalty

repealed: cancelled

trading posts: a store where fur trappers and hunters would sell their goods

Places to Remember

Willamette Valley: fertile valley in the state of Oregon

Oregon: western state on the coast of the Pacific Ocean

Louisiana Purchase: large territory President Jefferson bought from France

Salem: a city in Oregon

People to Remember

Thomas Jefferson: wrote the Declaration of Independence; third president

John McLoughlin: founder of Oregon

Father Francis Blanchet: founded the Saint Paul mission

Lewis and Clark: men who explored the land of the Louisiana Purchase

Lewis and Clark

Lewis and Clark explore the Louisiana Purchase

When Thomas Jefferson was the third president, the United States bought a very large area of land. This was called the Louisiana Territory. It was purchased from the ruler of France, Napoleon, in 1803. This purchase of land doubled the size of the United States.

President Jefferson sent Meriwether Lewis and William Clark to explore and map the Louisiana Territory. They went as far west as the Pacific Ocean.

John McLoughlin builds up a trading company

The area in the northwest that is now the states of Washington and Oregon was controlled by both the United States and England. Who would finally own the area would depend upon those who lived there. One man who lived there helped America's claim to the Northwest Territory. His name was John McLoughlin.

John McLoughlin was born in Canada in 1784. His family members were devout Catholics. John was the oldest son. He trained to be a doctor. However, when he was in his early twenties, he joined the North West Company. This was a trading company that bought furs from the trappers in the northwest and sold them to people in the east.

In 1821, the North West Company merged with the Hudson Bay Company. John McLoughlin took over the Columbia River section of the Company business in 1823. The huge area in which he was in charge of the trading business included what are now the states of Washington, Oregon, California, Idaho, Nevada, Utah, Colorado, Wyoming and parts of Montana. In this very large area, John McLoughlin became a very important businessman and citizen.

John McLoughlin developed a system by which his company controlled the fur trade. Mountain men and Indians explored and trapped animals in the Rocky Mountains. They brought their furs to John McLoughlin's North West Company. He set up a system of trading posts throughout the huge territory of the Northwest. He earned over a million dollars annually for his company.

John McLoughlin's fair and honest dealings with the Indians kept them peaceful. The white trappers were free to explore and open new territory.

John McLoughlin builds up the land

With his own hard-earned money, John McLoughlin built Fort Vancouver, and it was very successful. He developed a farm nearby so the fort could be independent. Some of the crops grown on the farm were wheat, barley, oats, peas, and potatoes. John McLoughlin had planted an orchard of apples, pears, and quince. He stocked the farm with horses, cattle, goats, sheep, and hogs.

Two sawmills and two flour mills were built on land near the farm. John McLoughlin opened new trade by selling flour to the Russians in Alaska and by selling wood to the Spanish in the Hawaiian Islands. He was always fair in his dealings with everyone. Being a good example to others was important to him. John McLoughlin showed how an honest, caring Catholic man could succeed and prosper in business and use his money to help others.

John McLoughlin helps Catholics

John McLoughlin encouraged French Canadian settlers, most of whom were Catholic, to come and settle in the United States. They worked on the farm and in the sawmills and flourmills. When there was no priest for Sunday Mass, they gathered at the mill to pray. They prayed for a priest.

One of the fur trappers had told John McLoughlin about a beautiful, fertile valley. It is now called the Willamette Valley. In 1829, John claimed the land at Willamette Falls, which is now a part of Oregon City. He established a settlement there.

Priests in Oregon

In 1841, Father de Smet came to Oregon for the first time. By 1843, Father had brought two priests and seven nuns to help in Oregon. The people's prayers were being answered.

Two priests, Father Francis Blanchet and Father Demus, finally came and founded a mission at Saint Paul on the Willamette River. This was the center of their work. They built a church and a school with the help of John McLoughlin, his fur trappers, and his Indian friends.

The Oregon Trail

The trip to Oregon from the east was a hard one. Settlers were forced to travel over the Oregon Trail. They needed to leave Independence, Missouri, by March if they were to arrive in Oregon by October. Most people traveled in covered wagons. They rolled their wagons across the Great Plains, over the Rocky Mountains, and across the Blue Mountain. When they reached an area called "The Dalles," they would transfer all their goods and equipment from their wagons onto rafts or barges. Then they would float down the Columbia River. This was a dangerous water passage to Willamette Valley.

John McLouglin helps needy settlers

In 1843, a group of 875 men, women, and children set out from Independence, Missouri. The wagon master was Peter Burnett. The fort commander at Independence said, "You know this is going to be a very long and hard trip. If any of you want to stay here in Missouri, you may."

Peter Burnett said, "The people on this wagon train know the trip will be hard. But they all want to go. They want a new life in the Oregon Territory."

The people did not know just how hard the trip would be. After six long months of terrible hardship, they arrived at Fort Vancouver. They were starving, sick, and exhausted. McLoughlin welcomed the settlers, and took pity on them. He gave them food, clothes, seed, farm equipment, and money. This act of charity would be repeated over and over again as more settlers arrived sick, weak, or without money.

Because England and the United States were arguing over who owned this territory, McLoughlin was ordered by his Hudson Bay Company not to help the settlers. However, he told his Company, "In good conscience, I cannot let men, women, and children starve. I must give help where help is needed. I cannot ignore human suffering."

John McLouglin is mistreated

John McLoughlin was forced to resign from the Hudson Bay Company in 1845. He went to live on the land he had claimed at Willamette Falls. He knew that this land would soon be added to the United States.

Sadly, a group of settlers John had helped caused him trouble. In 1841, John had encouraged a Protestant missionary to settle near what is now Salem, Oregon. When Oregon was added to the United States, the Protestant Missionary Society claimed that they owned the land John McLoughlin had developed. They claimed that John McLoughlin was an English citizen so he had no right to the land. They sent men to Washington, D.C., the capital of the United States, to claim John McLoughlin's own land.

McLoughlin wrote a strong letter to the American lawmakers. He said, "I have been condemned by the British for helping American settlers. I fed and clothed Americans. I helped them with farm equipment and money. Now I am accused of preventing Americans from settling in Oregon.

"I could not have done more for these settlers if they had been my own family. I helped keep peace so there would be no war between the Indians and the settlers, or between Britain and the United States. These accusations are a treatment I do not deserve. I expected better from the American government."

The Protestant Missionary Society put pressure on the American Congress. As a result, Congress passed a law that took the land away from McLoughlin. In spite of this wrong, John McLoughlin took an oath of allegiance to the United States. He became an American citizen.

A wrong is made right

In 1857, John McLoughlin became very ill. He died that September in Oregon City. Five years after his death, Congress cancelled the bad law they had passed. The land John worked so hard to develop was given back to his family.

John McLoughlin is honored

Thirty years after McLoughlin's death, his portrait was hung over the Speaker's desk in the Oregon Senate. Under the picture is the inscription "Founder of Oregon." In 1953, the state of Oregon placed a statue of John McLoughlin in the National Statuary Hall in Washington, D.C.

More important than these honors was the good example that John McLoughlin gave. Peter Burnett, the first governor of California, wrote a book called *The Path That Led a Protestant Lawyer to the Catholic Religion.* In his book, Burnett gives credit to John McLoughlin's constant charity and honest dealing. Burnett wrote, "I doubt I would ever have become a Catholic if I hadn't met John McLoughlin. How many other people were converted because of his actions, only God knows." John McLoughlin was a great American and a great Catholic.

Do You Remember?

1. Which president purchased the Louisiana Territory?

   _____

2. What area did Lewis and Clark explore?

   _____

3. What was the name of the valley that John McLoughlin developed?

   _____

4. How did settlers travel to Oregon?

   _____

5. Who passed a law that took away John McLoughlin's land?

   _____

6. Who was the first governor of California, converted by John McLoughlin's good example?

   _____

Map Study Skills

Look at a map of the United States. Find the following states:

Oregon	Idaho	Washington
California	Nevada	Utah
Colorado	Wyoming	Montana

Words to Remember

Redemptorists: religious order founded by Saint Alphonsus Liguori

Gaelic: an old form of the Irish language

boomtown: fast-growing town with many new people

canal: a man-made waterway used for traveling in a boat

diocese: an area over which a bishop is in charge of churches

Places to Remember

Bohemia: a part of the country in Europe called the Czech Republic

Buffalo: city in northwestern New York State

Hudson River: river in New York State

People to Remember

St. John Neumann (Noy man): Redemptorist priest; bishop of Philadelphia

Bishop Dubois (Doo Bwah): bishop of New York

Fr. John Neumann is made Bishop.

John Neumann tries to become a priest

John Neumann was born in 1811, in Bohemia, an area now called the Czech Republic in Europe. As a boy, John loved to read Bible stories. His mother teased him, "John, all you ever do is read the Bible." However, John did enjoy hunting and fishing with his brother. Later, he went to the seminary to study. Sadly, while John was there, the bishop canceled all the ordinations. He said there were too many priests in Bohemia.

John was disappointed. He asked the head of the seminary, "Would you please write to New York City for me? Would you ask Bishop Dubois if he will accept me and ordain me a priest?"

The Father superior agreed. "Yes, John. You will make a good priest. I will write tonight. I'm sure Bishop Dubois needs German-speaking priests in the United States."

John waited a long time for a reply. He waited so long that he almost ran out of money. He decided to take a ship to New York before his money was gone. He prayed that when he arrived, the bishop would welcome him.

John Neumann comes to the United States

The voyage was very long. The food on the ship was almost all gone. The drinking water turned bad. Storms tossed the ship in all directions. Finally, one night the lights of a city appeared. It was New York City! How happy all the passengers were!

John Neumann had little money when he arrived. He found a small inn. With his last few pennies, he rented a room for the night. The next morning, he walked to old St. Patrick's Cathedral in lower Manhattan in New York.

John knocked on the door of the rectory. The housekeeper answered. She said, "What can I do for you?" John looked dirty and ragged. She thought he was a beggar. He said, "I am John Neumann. I want to see Bishop Dubois. I want to be a priest."

John Neumann comes to the United States.

Bishop Dubois was surprised to hear John's voice at the door. He said, "Come in! Come in! We need priests. I just wrote to your religious superior. I told him you were welcome. The letter must have passed you on the ocean."

Bishop Dubois had a huge diocese in New York. He had mostly Irish priests. He had only three German-speaking priests, although he had many German-speaking Catholics asking for priests.

John Neumann becomes a priest

John Neumann entered the seminary where he studied for the sacrament of Holy Orders. He promised the Blessed Mother that he would say the Rosary every day. While he waited to be ordained, John taught the children of Saint Nicholas Church who would be receiving their First Holy Communion. He loved teaching the children.

Bishop Dubois ordained John in 1836 at St. Patrick's Cathedral in New York City. The next day, John said his first Mass at Saint Nicholas Church. Some of the children he had taught received their First Holy Communion.

Father Neumann prays.

That night, John wrote in his diary, "Oh, Jesus, You poured out the fullness of Your grace over me yesterday. You made me a priest. You gave me the power to offer You up to God the Father! Oh, God! This is too much for my soul!

"Angels of God, all you saints of Heaven, come down and adore my Jesus. What my heart says is only the imperfect echo of what Holy Church tells me to say.

"I will pray to You, Jesus, to give me holiness. I will pray to You to give all the living and the dead, pardon for their sins. Someday, may we all be together with You, Our Dearest God!"

Father Neumann goes to Buffalo, New York

The bishop of New York decided to send John Neumann to Buffalo, New York. The German-speaking people there needed a priest. John went up the Hudson River on a thirteen-hour boat trip to Albany, New York. The next day, he traveled three hours by train to Schenectady, New York. After this, Father Neumann traveled by barge on the Erie Canal. Three days later, the young priest arrived in Rochester, New York.

In Rochester, John met Father Prost, a Redemptorist priest. John was impressed with Father Prost's holiness. Later John Neumann would join the Redemptorist Order himself.

John continued his trip by spending two more days on the Erie Canal to travel to Buffalo. The canal had made Buffalo a boomtown. The pastor of the church in Buffalo greeted John saying, "I am so glad you are here! I can't keep up with all the work."

John Neumann becomes a Redemptorist priest

There were four hundred Catholic families spread over one hundred miles around Buffalo. John determined to visit every one as soon as he could. John worked hard in the Buffalo area for four years. However, after much prayer, John decided God wanted him to be a Redemptorist priest. He received permission from the bishop and left for Baltimore, Maryland.

In Baltimore, the Redemptorist priests would travel from Saint James Church to serve the needs of the German-speaking people as far south as Virginia, North Carolina, Kentucky, and Tennessee, and as far north as Ohio and Pennsylvania. In less than a year, ninety-nine babies were baptized. Fifty adult converts were baptized.

Children's catechism classes in German were started. Father Neumann wrote a catechism in German to use in these classes.

One day, John told his religious superior, "The children need Catholic schools. We need more than just catechism classes on Sunday." This became very important to John. From then on, whenever John built a church, he built a Catholic school right next to the church building.

Bishop Kendrick of Philadelphia watched all that Father Neumann had accomplished. The humble, saintly John Neumann seemed to reach even the most hardened heart. He was patient and charitable. Father Neumann would give his last dime to any poor person. He never said, "I can't do it." He always said, "With God's help, anything is possible."

Philadelphia gets a new bishop

Suddenly, the pope appointed Bishop Kendrick archbishop of Baltimore. This meant that Philadelphia needed a bishop. Bishop Kendrick suggested to the pope that Father John Neumann become the new bishop of Philadelphia. When John heard this, he was stunned. Father Neumann quickly walked over to the nuns who were teaching in his school. He said, "Sisters, please start praying. A disaster is about to befall the Church!" Mother Mary Joseph said, "What shall we pray for, Father?" He replied, "Pray they don't make me bishop of Philadelphia!"

Father of the Catholic Schools

God answered the nun's prayers in His own way. The pope made Father John Neumann the fourth bishop of Philadelphia. Under his care, the diocese of Philadelphia grew quickly. Bishop John Neumann built schools in every parish. Now that the Catholic schools were teaching the Faith to the children every day, many young people wanted to become priests and nuns.

Several orders of nuns and brothers came from Europe to teach in Bishop Neumann's schools. He also founded and supported six orders of American nuns. In time, with vocations coming from the students in the schools, there was no need to travel to Europe for priests and nuns.

Bishop Neumann works to protect the Church

Things were going well in Philadelphia, but not everything was good. There were some men who hated Catholics. These bad men even attacked the priests. They burned down several Catholic churches. Catholic men often had to stand outside and protect the churches during Mass. Sometimes anti-Catholic firemen would not put out the fires that burned the churches.

Sometimes Catholics argued with each other. The German Catholics wanted a German church. The Irish Catholics wanted their own Irish church, too. Bishop Neumann answered, "We are all Catholics. The Mass is in Latin so only the sermons are in German or Irish." In the end, everyone learned English and the priests gave the sermons in English.

Bishop Neumann hears confessions

Bishop Neumann liked to travel around his diocese. He loved to hear confessions and give absolution. He said, "It is wonderful to see souls come back to the state of grace."

In one small Pennsylvania town, the Irish immigrants spoke only Gaelic, an old form of the Irish language. An old woman came to confession. Bishop Neumann, who spoke German, French, Italian, Portuguese, and English, could not understand Gaelic. He could not give her absolution. So he went home and learned Gaelic.

The next year, the old woman came to confession again. The bishop heard her confession in Gaelic. She came out of the confessional smiling. She exclaimed, "Thanks be to God! Now we have a real Irish bishop!"

Bishop Neumann starts the Forty Hours Devotion

Nothing was too much for Bishop Neumann to do for the souls in his care. He wanted to inspire more reverence for Christ in the Blessed Sacrament. He began the Forty Hours Devotion in all the Philadelphia churches.

Forty Hours Devotion began with a procession of First Communion children leading the rest of the parish after the last Mass on Sunday. The Blessed Sacrament was exposed in the monstrance on the high altar. People came all day and all night to adore Jesus in the Blessed Sacrament. On Tuesday, forty hours later, there was Benediction and ending songs. Then Jesus was put back in the tabernacle.

The last days of Bishop Neumann

In January of 1860, Bishop Neumann became very ill. The doctors told him to rest. However, he had a chalice which had to be sent to a poor priest in western Pennsylvania. He walked to the post office. On the way back, he collapsed. He was taken to a nearby house. He died in the house of a stranger. Only God and His angels were there to comfort him.

On January 6, 1860, John Neumann, the beloved Bishop of Philadelphia was buried. He had the largest funeral in the history of the city. He was buried in St. Peter's Church in Philadelphia. All the schoolchildren, priests, nuns, brothers, and other

St. John Neumann gives Benediction at the close of Forty Hours Devotion.

people rich and poor, lined the street as his body was carried to the cathedral to be buried. The poor of Philadelphia had lost their best friend.

St. John Neumann, help us to have a strong devotion to Christ in the Blessed Sacrament. Help us to care for the poor.

Do You Remember?

1. What were the six languages John Neumann learned to speak?

   _____

   _____

2. Where was John Neumann ordained? _____

   _____

3. What Order of priests did he join? _____

4. For what city was John Neumann the bishop?

   _____

5. What did John Neumann build next to a new church?

   _____

6. What special devotion did John Neumann introduce?

   _____

Map Study Skills

1. On a map of the United States, find the following cities:

   New York, Albany, Rochester, and Buffalo in New York;

   Philadelphia, Pennsylvania; Baltimore, Maryland.

2. On a map of the United States, find the following states:

   Virginia, Tennessee, North Carolina, Kentucky, Ohio, Pennsylvania.

Chapter 16

Nuns in the Civil War and After

Words to Remember

chaos: state of complete disorder

cholera: a deadly disease

assassinate: to kill an important public figure

fanatics: those who follow a cause violently, often with blind devotion

Reconstruction: the reorganization of the South after the Civil War

vengeance: punishment inflicted to repay an injury or wrong

Places to Remember

Leavenworth: a city in the state of Kansas

Trinidad: town in the state of Colorado

Albuquerque: city in the state of New Mexico

Santa Fe: city in New Mexico

People to Remember

Bishop Lamy: saintly bishop of Santa Fe, New Mexico

Sister Blandina: Sister of Charity in New Mexico and Colorado

Billy the Kid: outlaw who protected Sister Blandina

Cavalry charge by Southern soldiers during the Civil War

Nuns work as nurses during the Civil War

The Civil War or The War Between the States was one of the darkest times in American history. Wars happen because of sin. Men are not perfect. Cruelty and greed are what usually start wars.

Some Catholics were on the side of the North, some Catholics were on the side of the South. This war caused grief among members of one and the same family. It is difficult to practice virtue with so much sadness and suffering all around. The best example of charity was the nursing work of Catholic sisters or nuns. There is a statue in Washington D.C. dedicated to the "Nuns of the Battlefield." Over six hundred Catholic sisters volunteered as nurses during the war.

Sisters of Charity, Sisters of Mercy, Sisters of Our Lady of Mount Carmel, Ursuline Sisters, Sisters of the Holy Cross, Dominican Sisters, Sisters of Providence, Poor Sisters of Saint Francis, and the Sisters of Saint Joseph all worked close to the battlefield, caring for the wounded and the dying. Over 600,000 men died, and many more were wounded during the war from 1861 to 1865.

The community that sent the most Sisters to help was the Daughters of Charity of St. Vincent de Paul. Over two hundred and thirty nuns of this Order volunteered to help the wounded and dying soldiers. They earned the name of "Angels of Mercy."

The Catholic Sisters did all the nursing during the war. After doing all they could to save a man's life, the nuns would pray for him. If the soldier was Catholic and there was no priest, the nuns would say, "Young man, examine your conscience. Tell God you are sorry for your sins. Let us say the Act of Contrition together." So they helped many soldiers to die in the state of grace.

The good example of the nursing nuns brought many Catholics back to the Church. Their example converted many non-Catholics. The Sisters showed humility, courage, and charity. They changed the minds and the hearts of many who hated the Church.

Catholic Sisters nursed the wounded soldiers.

Reconstruction in the South

The problems between the North and the South continued after the war ended. President Abraham Lincoln was assassinated just after the war. His vice president, Andrew Johnson, became president. Sadly, he could not heal the hatred the war caused.

In the South, the time after the war was very hard indeed. Most of the fighting had been in the South. Many families lost their homes, their land, and their jobs. They lost their fathers, sons, and husbands. After the war, many Southern families moved out to the western states to start their lives over again.

Unlike some, the Catholic Church showed love and unity. In 1866, right after the war ended, a Church Council was held in Baltimore. Priests and bishops from both the North and the South worked and prayed together. This was a shining example of how Christians should act.

Jefferson Davis had been the president of the South's Confederate States of America. His wife said, "I am left in poverty. No one in my own religion comes to help me or my children. Only Catholic Sisters help me to care for my children. God bless them all."

Bishop Lamy of Santa Fe

The courage that took the Sisters into the face of death on the battlefield also took them west to face Indian attacks and hardships. The nuns did not go west for the reasons of the average American. They did not go west to make a fortune, start a new life, or escape from the problems of the war. The nuns selflessly dedicated their lives to saving souls for Jesus Christ. That was their only reason for moving west with the pioneers.

Bishop Lamy of Santa Fe, New Mexico, left Fort Leavenworth, Kansas, in 1867, with a wagon train full of supplies. He had four Sisters of Loretto returning with him. They had volunteered to teach in his schools. Suddenly, the bishop ordered the wagons to circle. The Kiowa Indians were attacking.

During the attack, a sister crawled out from under the wagon to pull back a man who had been shot. The others nursed those who were hurt. Then one of the sisters collapsed. She had cholera, a very bad disease. Two more people collapsed and died. As the sun went down, the Indians withdrew. At dawn, they attacked again.

By this time, the people were very thirsty. Bishop Lamy realized they could not fight another day. That night, the bishop ordered fires put out for the night. The Indians went to sleep. The wagons slipped away quickly and quietly under the cover of darkness and God's protection. Two months later, they arrived in Santa Fe. Most trips west were just as difficult as this one.

The settlers flee the Indian attack.

Sister Blandina Segale heads west

One of the most extraordinary pioneers was Sister Blandina Segale. Sister Blandina was born in Italy in 1850. Her parents brought her to the United States to Cleveland, Ohio, when she was only five years old. At the age of eighteen, Blandina became a Sister of Charity.

In 1872, Sister Mary Joseph, her religious superior, said, "Sister Blandina, you are going to Trinidad. Sister Theresa will help you pack. You are going on the train tomorrow, alone."

Sister Blandina asked, "Yes, Sister. But where is Trinidad?" Sister Mary Joseph explained, "Sister Blandina, you are going west, to Trinidad, in the state of Colorado."

The next morning, Sister Blandina left for Colorado. On the train, she sat next to a woman. The lady asked, "Where are you going?" Sister Blandina replied, "Trinidad, Colorado."

The lady gasped, "Sister, do you know Trinidad is one of the most wicked towns in the West? All the outlaws gather there. How can you go to such a place?" Sister Blandina answered, "God is sending me to convert the outlaws as well as the law-abiding citizens."

Sister Blandina meets an outlaw

When Sister Blandina arrived in Trinidad, not only did she convert the outlaws, she also started the first free school in Colorado. Sister Blandina started an academy for the wealthy girls as well. She started a hospital for everyone. She was responsible for bringing civilization, as well as the Catholic Faith, to the most wicked city in the West.

When new nuns came to replace her, Sister Blandina moved to Santa Fe, New Mexico. She worked over twenty years in New Mexico and Colorado. She made friends with the outlaws and the law-abiding citizens. Anything that needed to be done, she accomplished it, even if she had to do it herself.

When Billy the Kid's gang robbed the town bank, one of his men was shot. None of the town doctors would help the outlaw. Sister Blandina took him to the jail and bandaged his wounds. Billy the Kid came back to get his man. He said, "Thanks for the help, Sister. I'm going to kill those doctors. Is there anything I can do for you?"

Sister Blandina replied, "Yes. Leave quietly and don't kill anyone." So Billy the Kid did leave, without killing anyone.

Billy the Kid left without killing anyone.

Sister Blandina stands up for the truth

One time, Sister stopped a man from being hanged. Several times, Sister stopped the Apache Indians from going on the warpath. Sister Blandina begged for money from miners to build a hospital. Sometimes, she and her sisters built coffins to bury poor people when there was no money.

When the people in one town refused to help Sister Blandina pull down the remains of a school building, the nuns started pulling it down themselves. The women of the town were shocked. That shamed their men into helping Sister Blandina. Later, the men built a new school building.

In Albuquerque, New Mexico, the town politicians wanted Sister Blandina to stop wearing her religious habit while she was teaching. They said her religious dress interfered with the separation of church and state. Sister Blandina said, "My habit is a sign to everyone that I am a bride of Christ. I will not take it off. Find someone else to run your school." She left.

Sister Blandina was always determined. She knew God was good. God had sent her west to accomplish His will. For her, no labor was too hard, no sacrifice was considered impossible.

With the help of God, all things can be accomplished. This is what Sister Blandina and the many Sisters who followed her example believed. They helped build churches as well as schools, hospitals, and orphanages. Their faith and courage helped build our western United States. Catholic religious Sisters helped bring civilization out of chaos.

Christ, Prince of Peace, help us to love one another.

Do You Remember?

1. Where is the statue of the Nuns of the Battlefield?

   _____

2. What bishop was attacked by Indians?

   _____

3. Where was Sister Blandina sent?

   _____

Map Study Skills

On a map of the United States, locate the following states:

Colorado and New Mexico.

Chapter 17

Two Holy Nuns Help the Forgotten People

Words to Remember

orphanage: home for children who do not have parents

integrated: united together

Places to Remember

Richmond: capital of the state of Virginia

James River: river in Virginia

Chicago: largest city in the state of Illinois

Seattle: city in Washington State

Omaha: city in the state of Nebraska

People to Remember

Saint Frances Xavier Cabrini: founded Missionary Sisters of the Sacred Heart

Saint Katharine Drexel: founded Sisters of the Blessed Sacrament

Bishop James O'Connor: bishop of Omaha, Nebraska

Contessa Desmala: helped pay to start an orphanage

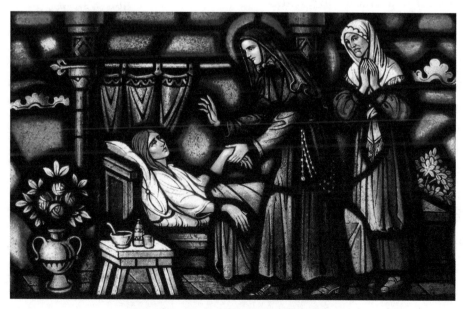

Mother Cabrini tends the sick.

By the 1900s, the forgotten people in America were the poor immigrants, the American Indians, and the newly-freed Black people. Two amazing nuns would befriend these three groups of forgotten people. These nuns understood that the key to becoming part of society is the Catholic faith and education.

Young Frances Cabrini

Frances Xavier Cabrini was born in Italy in 1850. She was the youngest of thirteen children. Her family was deeply religious.

In those days, no one had radio or television or computers. They had not been invented yet. At night, one member of the Cabrini family would read from a book about missionaries. These stories were exciting to young Frances. She wanted to be a missionary to help people learn about Jesus and His true Church.

Frances' older sister, Rose, was a teacher. She taught and trained young Frances. Frances knew her prayers by age three. She learned the Stations of the Cross and the mysteries of the Rosary by age six. Frances prayed that she would become a missionary nun.

Frances dreamed of being a missionary like Francis Xavier.

When Frances played with her dolls, she dressed them up as nuns. She made paper boats, put them in the nearby river, and pretended to sail to China. One day, she fell into the river. After that, she did not sail any more paper boats.

Frances' parents decided she should be a teacher. When she was eighteen, her parents sent her to a teacher training school. She did as her parents asked. The year she graduated and passed the exams, both her parents died. She was very sad and had many Masses offered for them.

Frances becomes a nun

Since her parents had died, Frances decided to try to become a nun. Several orders of nuns refused to take Frances into the convent because her health was not good. When she spoke to her parish priest, he asked her, "Frances, will you manage our parish orphanage? You can live there like a nun."

Frances said, "I will try to help. I would like living as a nun."

Frances asked seven other women friends to join her in helping the children in the orphanage. In 1877, however, she started planning on starting an order of missionary nuns. The bishop told her, "You want to be a missionary? I don't know of any order of missionary nuns! But you can try to start your own!"

Frances and her seven followers moved to an old abandoned Franciscan priory in a nearby Italian town. For three years, Frances worked on writing the Rule of the community. The main work of the Sisters would be the Catholic education of girls. The name was to be the Missionary Sisters of the Sacred Heart.

Mother Cabrini opened a free school and an orphanage in Rome. The pope gave approval to her new community and their Rule. Though she wanted to go to China, Mother Cabrini was then advised by her bishop to go to America. They needed the help of the nuns to teach the Italian immigrant children.

Finally, her bishop advised, "Ask the pope where you should go."

Mother Cabrini comes to America

Frances went to Pope Leo XIII. The pope encouraged her to go to America. Francis believed that the pope's word was God's will. She would take her nuns to America.

In 1889, Frances and nine religious Sisters arrived in New York City. The bishop who had invited them had no place for them to live. He said, "Sisters, I am sorry. We have no building for you. If you wish to return to Italy, I will pay your way back."

Mother Cabrini said, "No, Your Excellency! The pope said we should come here and here we will stay."

Almost immediately, Frances met Contessa Desmala who found a house for the nuns. She helped Mother Cabrini and her sisters start an orphanage. The order began to grow. They moved to West Park on the Hudson River. This became their motherhouse where young girls learned how to be faithful Missionary Sisters of the Sacred Heart of Jesus.

Mother Cabrini and her nuns started working among the Italian immigrants, but soon her work spread to help all God's poor whether or not they were Italian. She and her Sisters started schools, orphanages, and hospitals from New York to Chicago and from New Orleans to Seattle. Her missionary travels even took her to Central and South America. She started fifty schools and twenty hospitals. Mother Cabrini's community of nuns grew from the original seven to over one thousand nuns.

Mother Cabrini helped the poor and the immigrants.

St. Frances Cabrini's earthly work comes to a close

Frances became ill in 1910. She kept on working until she collapsed. She died in December of 1917 in one of her Chicago convents. Her body is enshrined in the Chapel of Cabrini Memorial School at Port Washington, New York. Mother Cabrini was canonized in 1946. Though born in Italy, she had become an American citizen. She was the first U.S. citizen to be canonized a saint.

Saint Frances Cabrini, help the poor.

Young Katharine Drexel

Mother Katharine Drexel was a friend of Mother Cabrini. Katharine was born to a wealthy banking family in Philadelphia in 1858. Her mother died five days after her birth. She was raised by a stepmother, though Katharine always called her Mother. She and her older sister, Elizabeth, and a younger sister, Louise, were all very close.

Their stepmother taught the three girls at home. One of the large upstairs rooms was turned into a classroom. It had desks, many books, maps, and a blackboard. The girls had tutors for Latin and French. Mrs. Drexel taught them religion, composition, literature, and history. Their father, Mr. Drexel, taught them math and science. He made sure they learned bookkeeping and banking, also.

Saint Katharine Drexel Shrine

The girls spent the summers on their father's large farm in western Pennsylvania. They called it Saint Michael's. There was a large statue of Saint Michael at the entrance. It was here that Katharine first started teaching. There was a chapel in the house. During the summer, Sunday Mass was offered there. On Sunday afternoon, the three girls taught catechism to the children of the farm workers.

Katharine starts an order of nuns

In Pennsylvania, Katharine met Father James O'Connor, the parish priest. He encouraged Katharine to start a community of nuns. Father would later become the bishop of Omaha, Nebraska. For almost all of Katharine Drexel's life, Father O'Connor was her spiritual director and helped her grow closer to God.

When Katharine was fourteen years old, her mother became ill with cancer. Katharine nursed her mother until she died. From this experience, Katharine learned the importance of suffering. She watched her mother offer up her pain for the poor souls in Purgatory. From her mother's sufferings and death, Katharine learned there was more to life than money and material things. From her father also, Katharine learned that money and material things were given to people so they could help others in need.

One year later, Mr. Drexel said to his daughters one night, "I have written my will. If anything happens to me, no one will marry you for your money. After ten percent of my estate has been given to charity, the rest will be held in trust. You will each receive part of the interest on the trust. If one of you dies without a child, the others will split her share of the interest. When all of you die, the trust will be divided among the charities I name."

The girls were stunned. Katharine said, "Daddy, don't talk like that. We don't want to think about your death." Mr. Drexel had been wise. Two years later, he died.

Their father had trained his daughters well. They each used their inheritance wisely. Each daughter had a special charity. Elizabeth started Saint John's Orphanage and Saint Francis Industrial School in Eddington, Pennsylvania. Louise married Colonel Morell. She and her husband founded Saint Emma's Industrial School for Black boys, thirty miles from Richmond, Virginia.

Katharine used her money for many charities. She was especially interested in the Indians and the blacks. On a visit to Europe, the three sisters were granted a private audience with Pope Leo XIII. When Katharine complained about the poor treatment given Indians and Blacks, Pope Leo said, "Start a community of nuns and care for them yourself."

Katharine spoke to her spiritual advisor, Bishop O'Connor. "The pope says I should start a community of nuns." He replied, "I believe you have the ability to do it. There will be much sacrifice. You are used to living well. Can you live in poverty? Think about it."

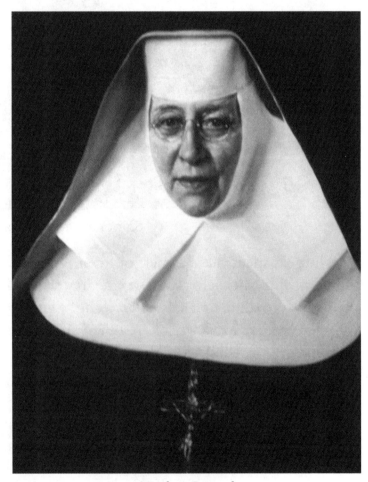

Mother Drexel

After much prayer, Katharine decided to start the Sisters of the Blessed Sacrament for Indians and Colored People. The community of nuns who joined her took four vows: poverty, chastity, obedience, and a special vow to serve the Indians and Black people all their lives. Since Katharine was in charge, the nuns called her Mother Drexel.

Mother Drexel helps the Indians and the Blacks

Mother Drexel traveled west and established twenty Indian missions from South Dakota to New Mexico. The Mission of St. Katharine's was at Wounded Knee in South Dakota. When the Indians there revolted because of the harsh treatment of the government, the chief said to his Indian friends, "Mother Katharine has always been good to us. She has kept all her promises. We must not damage Mother Katharine's Mission."

The nuns did not leave the mission during the Indian revolt. Everything around them was destroyed during the Indian revolt. Yet, neither the Indians nor the soldiers touched Mother Drexel's Mission.

As the community of nuns grew, Mother Drexel began her

Mother Drexel helped the Indians and the Blacks.

work among the Blacks, who in those days were called "Colored." She purchased land across the James River to start a school for girls. She named it Saint Francis de Sales School. The school was very successful.

One day, on a train ride to her Saint Francis de Sales School, Mother Drexel saw a gold cross gleaming in the sun. She said, "Sister Mary, is there a Catholic church in Columbia, Virginia?" Her companion replied, "No, Mother, there isn't a church between Lynchburg and Richmond."

When they arrived at the school, Mother Drexel asked a Black girl from Columbia, Virginia, if there was a church there. The girl answered, "Yes. My father takes care of it."

Later, the girl took them to visit the church in Virginia. The altar had clean linens and flowers. The church was spotless. The girl's father said, "I take care of it. I pray every day for a priest to come."

Mother Drexel appealed to the bishop. Finally, a priest was sent to offer Mass at the church. The nuns came to give instruction. Soon many of the people in the area became Catholic.

Mother Drexel starts schools and colleges

Mother Drexel knew education was the way to help the poor, the Indians, and the Blacks obtain good jobs. Mother Drexel herself established Xavier University in New Orleans. Mother Drexel also started five schools in Harlem in New York City. She opened other schools across the southern states.

When the Supreme Court of the United States of America ruled that schools should be integrated with all children, whether black or white, Mother Drexel opened her schools to all children, no matter what the color of their skin. She worked long and hard for the poorest of God's children.

Mother Drexel lived to be ninety-seven years old! The Sisters of the Blessed Sacrament for Indians and Colored People asked the pope for her beatification. This banker's daughter, who gave up everything to serve Christ's poor, has been declared a saint.

St. Katharine Drexel, pray for us.

Do You Remember?

1. Where was Frances Xavier Cabrini born? _____

2. Where did Frances want to go to be a missionary? _____

3. Where did Frances first land in America? _____

4. Where was Mother Katharine Drexel born? _____

5. What pope told her to found a religious community? _____

6. What university in New Orleans did Mother Drexel found?

_____

Map Study Skills

On a map of the United States, find the following states:

North Dakota   South Dakota   Nevada

Georgia   Nebraska.

Chapter 18

Irish Christian Brothers Come to America

Words to Remember

Monsignor: title of honor given by the Church to certain priests

rectory: home where the priest lives

vocation: the state in life to which a person is called by God

People to Remember

Archbishop James Whitfield: archbishop of Baltimore

Monsignor James Power: pastor of All Saints parish in New York City

Brother Titus Frisby: an Irish Christian Brother who came to New York

John Cardinal Farley: archbishop of New York

Brother Edmund Rice: founder of the Irish Christian Brothers

Iona College in New Rochelle, NY, started by the Christian Brothers in 1940

Blessed Brother Edmund Rice

God calls men to different religious vocations. Not all men are called to be priests. Some are called to be a religious "Brother," that is, a member of a religious community. If the community is an active one, the Brother usually works as a teacher, a nurse, or a counselor.

Many religious communities came to America in the 1800s. The Irish Christian Brothers, founded by Brother Edmund Rice, was one of the communities which came to America and greatly influenced many Americans.

Pope Pius VII approved the Christian Brothers in 1820.

The Christian Brothers come to America

It all started when Archbishop Whitfield of Baltimore wrote to Brother Edmund Rice in 1828, asking if the Irish Christian Brothers could come to America. The archbishop wrote, "We have free schools for boys. They are under the care of regular teachers. However, the teachers are very, very different from pious religious men, or Brothers."

As much as Brother Rice wanted to send members of his young community, he was unable to do so. Anti-Catholic England had passed a law that forbade young Catholic men to enter religious organizations. For several years, there were no new vocations.

From 1838 to 1862, for almost twenty-five years, there was massive immigration of poor Irish families to the United States. Because of the terrible persecution of Catholics by the English, thousands were escaping from Ireland. Several bishops in the United States asked the Irish Christian Brothers to come and teach, but the vocations were still too few.

The bishops turned to French congregations of Brothers. In the 1840s, the De La Salle Brothers, the Holy Cross Brothers, the Sacred Heart Brothers, and the Xaverian Brothers came to the United States. Each of these congregations grew as young American boys learned their Catholic Faith and later became Brothers themselves. Despite this, and the number of nuns who came to America, there were still not enough vocations to fill the need for teachers in the Catholic schools. Some Catholic children were forced to attend public schools where many Protestants of English descent treated the Catholics as enemies. As Bishop Neumann said of these schools, "Public schools teach Catholic children Protestant ideas." Many lost their Catholic faith.

Monsignor James Power and Brother Titus Frisby

It seems God wanted the Irish Christian Brothers to be in the United States of America. Two men helped make this happen. They were Monsignor James Power and Brother Titus Frisby.

James Power was born in Waterford, Ireland. As a young priest, he had come to New York to serve the ever-growing Catholic population. He became pastor of All Saints Church, a growing parish in New York City.

Brother Titus Frisby was an Irish Christian Brother. He was sent to New York in 1903 to beg for funds for his Order. Of all the Brothers who were sent, Brother Titus was the most successful. He had a bright and lively personality. He had what the Irish called "a way about him." Everyone liked Brother Titus, especially the children.

Brother Titus went to Monsignor Power and asked him, "May I stay in your rectory while I am in the United States?" Monsignor Power agreed. The two men became good friends. When Brother Titus came in at night, Monsignor Power would ask, "How did it go today?" Titus would reach into his pocket and pull out a wad of money. Then he would reach in his other pocket and pull out more money. Both men would thank God for providing money to help educate poor boys.

Brother Titus would say, "God has been very good to us this day." He knew that being a good money-raiser was only a small part of his job. Being a good, prayerful, and holy Christian Brother was the most important part of his vocation.

Monsignor Power asked, "Brother Titus, do you think the Irish Christian Brothers would come and teach at my school?"

Brother Titus replied, "I will write and ask. I think that our community would be good for your school. I also think there are many undiscovered vocations here in America."

The Brother Superior of the Christian Brothers in Ireland agreed to send four Brothers. Monsignor Power wrote his archbishop, "The Sisters can no longer handle the boys' section of sixth through eighth grade in our All Saints School. The Irish Christian Brothers have agreed to come. Pope Leo XIII invited them to teach in the English schools for the children in Rome. Pope Pius X, now reigning, has high praise for the Brothers' teaching."

The archbishop was happy and agreed. He was especially happy when Monsignor Power pointed out that a good percentage of the boys in the Irish Christian Brothers'

New York City in 1903 was an exciting city.

schools became priests. The archbishop believed that with a good Catholic education, more Catholic boys would become priests.

Interior of Old St. Patrick's Cathedral in New York City

In 1906, Brother Ryan and three other brothers came to New York. The Irish Christian Brothers finally started what would turn out to be a very successful community in the United States. Monsignor Power was very friendly and helpful to the Brothers.

The boys in the Catholic schools were poor and rough. They were not so willing to be taught anything. The boys would often cause trouble, trying to test the Christian Brothers to see what would happen. The Brothers knew how to teach the boys, however. Brother Ryan and the other Brothers soon were able to train the boys to obey. Order and learning soon became a part of the boys' lives.

Good grades

At that time, all the boys from working class families went to work after elementary school because families were poor. Good marks on final exams helped the boys to find better jobs. The Brothers knew how to teach the boys to take final exams. Every boy in the graduating class obtained a high mark on the arithmetic part of the exam as a result of the help from the Christian Brothers.

Because the grades for the boys had been so low in the past, Dr. Skinner of the New York State Department of Education thought the boys had cheated on the exams. He came to the school and examined the boys himself. They answered everything correctly.

Dr. Skinner was very impressed. He became a lifelong supporter of the Irish Christian Brothers. He was particularly helpful when the Brothers started a high school and wanted it approved by the state of New York.

Determined to stay in the United States, all the Brothers became citizens. Soon, they established the Irish Christian Brothers Institute so that they could obtain donations for their schools. Monsignor Power helped the Christian Brothers to establish their own high school, which opened in 1909.

Brother Ignatius and Brother Ryan

Brother Ignatius was sent to help with the new high school opened by the Irish Christian Brothers. Brother Ignatius and Brother Ryan worked well together. The two Brothers were well educated and were able to plan for future schools. They were able to solve many problems and to overcome difficulties. In one year alone, several elementary and high schools were started in New York because of Brother Ignatius and Brother Ryan.

For almost sixty years, Brother Ignatius and Brother Ryan served their Christian Brothers community. They established a novitiate, a place to train new Brothers in New Rochelle, north of New York City. By the late 1920s, the Christian Brothers had so many vocations for Brothers that they no longer needed help from Ireland.

Brother Ignatius helped the Christian Brothers start schools all over the country. The Brothers looked for a permanent place for their headquarters. When they finally found good property, the owner would not sell it to Catholics. Brother Ignatius said, "If God wants us to have the property, it will be ours."

The owner suddenly found himself desperately in need of cash. Then he was happy to sell to the Christian Brothers. The money came from grateful former students, good Catholic friends, and Monsignor Power.

Christian Brothers in the West

The Christian Brothers were active in the West also. The bishop of Seattle, Washington, asked the Christian Brothers to open an orphanage for boys. The Christian Brothers responded by starting the Brisco Orphanage in 1914. Brother Rupert was the famous Superior at the orphanage. He served the poor boys with love and dedication for twenty-seven years, until his death.

The Brothers also opened a high school in Seattle, and before 1924, Boys Central High School in Butte, Montana, was also started.

The successful community of Christian Brothers in America owed much to Monsignor Power. When he died in 1928, the Brothers lost their best friend. There were over one hundred and fifty Brothers in America by then.

New York

All Hallows High School in New York had been started in two old brownstone houses. In 1929, the Brothers moved to a new building in the Bronx. Then the Depression hit. Many people lost their money.

The Brothers used old buildings to start Power Memorial High School. They arranged with pastors to pay some of the tuition for the poor boys from their parishes. That way, many more boys were able to attend high school. Over two hundred boys were enrolled in the Power Memorial High School.

In 1940, the Irish Christian Brothers opened Iona College in New York State. The final school opened by the Irish Christian Brothers was Cardinal Farley Military Academy on Long Island, in New York.

The good Catholic education given to Catholic immigrant

New St. Patrick's Cathedral, New York

children helped them go far in society. Vocations to the priesthood and the religious life were the crowning jewels in the reputation of these teaching Brothers. Many boys grew up as solid practicing Catholics, attending Mass and going to Confession frequently. Many laymen raised their families in the Catholic Faith they learned from the Christian Brothers. Only in Heaven will we know the full extent of the influence and good example of these heroic Christian Brothers.

St. Joseph, help all the Catholic Brothers in their work.

Do You Remember?

1. Who first asked the Irish Christian Brothers to come to America?

    _____

2. What was the name of the priest who helped them in America?

    _____

3. What was the first school they served in New York?

    _____

Map Study Skills

On a map of the United States, find the following places:

The city of Chicago, Illinois

The state of Washington

The city of Seattle, Washington

Annunciation Window from St. Patrick's Cathedral in New York City